ACTUALLY, I CAN

Rewriting the Rules of Resilience

by

Nika Stewart

the publishing CIRCLE.

Actually, I Can:
Rewriting the Rules of Resilience

FIRST EDITION

ISBN 978-1-955018-46-3 (PAPERBACK)
ISBN 978-1-955018-47-0 (LARGE-PRINT PAPERBACK)
ISBN 978-1-955018-48-7 (HARDCOVER)
ISBN 978-1-955018-49-4 (E-BOOK)

This book is dedicated to the vibrant rebel spirit in you.

Think you can't transform a daunting challenge into your most spectacular, awe-inspiring, life-revolutionizing, cheer-worthy triumph?

Actually, you can.

TABLE OF CONTENTS

Praise for Actually, I Can.................................... *ix*

Acknowledgements ....*xiii*

Intro..1

Let's Start With the Good News 10

Pamphlets...12

Ground Zero—The Defining Moment 16

Choosing a Different Lens 22

Too Busy For Your Cancer......................................29

Choose Happy? 34

Flying Baby Elephant 38

Snap! A Biopsy Ballet..40

Post Needle Gunslinger 42

Just a Haircut 47

Blissfully Ignorant 51

The War Kitchen 53

Adversity Dodge Ball...60

Teeny Tiny Cancer Dot 64

A Real Biopsy 70

Harnessing My Power..73

The Big Reveal...78

Make That A Double...82

Find The Funny...91

Mastectomy 99

Empowered Healing: An Unconventional Checklist 103

My Expected Finale 107

Let's Go Home And Heal 111

Borrowing Power 113

The Results Are In! 116

Put Down The Load 121

Dance In The Rain 126

Embracing The "and"™ 130

I Can't Plan Boobs, So Let's Plan Hair 134

Righting My Story 139

Locks And Docs: Gearing Up For The Road Ahead 147

Port Of Call: Another Surgical Stopover 151

Chem-Huh?-Therapy 157

Dancing With The (Red) Devil 160

Rating The Wretchedness 167

Gratitude In The Darkness 170

Losing Locks, Gaining Giggles 172

Dancing Shaving In The Rain 178

Buzz! A Baldheaded Ballet 180

Releasing Perfection 185

Mirror Images 192

Finding Blessings 195

Tell Me A Joke 197

The Antidote To Adversity 203

A Tiktok Obsession Is Born 208

Lock Down That Attitude...210

Turn Whine Into Shine 213

Release The Perfect Image..215

Can't Hold This Beach Ball Down 218

Transitioning To Taxol: Silver Linings In Every Syringe....220

Along For The Ride..225

Pandemic Parodies...228

Find The Funny Sidebars?..233

Pints Of Positivity: Savoring Small Joys 237

One To Go: The Countdown Ballet................................242

No Bell To Ring, But 246

I May Have Lost A Lot...251

Hit The Road, Chuck...254

Self-Made Woman..256

Radiation Readiness...258

Dancing With Lymphedema..261

Whine Not?...265

Breast Cancer Awareness Month....................................268

Under Re-Construction..272

Curveballs And Comebacks 276

Braless To Flawless 278

Back To The Front...281

Good News, Bad News..285

Creating Your Own Milestones......................................291

Playing Games...299

About the Author 302

PRAISE FOR ACTUALLY, I CAN

". . . practical wisdom for anyone navigating life's unexpected hurdles. With sincerity, lots of humor and grace, Nika invites readers to reflect on their own challenges and empowers them to confront adversity with a resilient spirit. This book is a testament to the human capacity for transformation and the ability to discover light in the most unexpected places."
Vanessa Coppes, *BELLA Magazine*

~~

"A must-read for anyone seeking to navigate life's ups and downs with a lighter heart and a brighter outlook." Dawn Andrews, Founder FreeRangeThinking, Business Strategist

~~

"This book is an inspiring, eye-opening, and hilarious guide to finding light in life's darkest moments. It's the book we ALL need so we can show up and get more GOOD into the world!" Molly Mahoney, AI & Business Growth Strategist

~~

"A compelling and joyful guide to thriving amidst life's biggest storms. Nika's story shows us the power of laughter as a tool for healing and growth. I loved the small vignette style chapters (and titles)—reminded me of Steve Martin's writing, albeit a much more serious topic, but just as funny!" Jennifer Dunham, Founder of Happinessmatters.com

"This book redefines resilience. It's a powerful testament to finding happiness and humor, even when life takes unexpected turns." Elizabeth K. Goede, Founder Ratliff Consulting, AI and Brand Strategist

"Actually I Can is a mix of laughter and resilience and reality and gratitude and all the things that get wrapped up when you're in the midst of unexpected challenges. You don't have to have cancer to be inspired by Nika. From Adversity Dodgeball to Pints of Positivity you're sure to find applicable life lessons on every page."
Catherine Avery, 8-year cancer survivor

"This book made me laugh at the oddest moments and I loved it—it made my soul smile." Michelle Riley, Horticulturist

"*Actually I Can* is a must-read for those seeking to enrich their lives with greater laughter and resilience, offering a heartwarming, inspiring journey of transforming life's challenges into triumphs with humor and courage. Nika's captivating story illuminates the path to overcoming adversity with a sparkling blend of wit and wisdom." Ginna Tassanelli, Visibility Strategist & Founder of HYPE Media

~~~

"When it comes to handling setbacks, we can cry. We can yell. We can learn. We can laugh. And we can grow. Nika's book teaches us how to do all of that with grace, grit, and gumption!" Deborah Grayson Riegel, author, *Go to Help: 36 Ways to Offer, Ask for, and Accept Help*

~~~

"A fantastic blend of wit, wisdom, and warmth, 'Actually I Can' is an uplifting exploration of life's trials and triumphs. Nika's story is a powerful example of how a positive outlook and a sense of humor can transform adversity into an opportunity for personal growth and joy. An essential read for any and everyone looking to infuse their life with a bit more laughter and resilience." Stephanie Young, Executive Assistant

~~~

"Nika has always provided valuable ideas on how people can grow their businesses by stepping out of their comfort zones and building an online presence. But with 'Actually I Can,' she shares powerful advice on how not just to survive, but thrive, when life throws you for a curve." Larry Hoffer, Nonprofit Association Executive

~~~

"A life-affirming journey that brilliantly intertwines humor with healing. 'Actually I Can' is a must-read for anyone seeking joy in the face of adversity." Jessica Fein, author: *Breath Taking: A Memoir of Family, Dreams, and Broken Genes*

~~~

"Nika's incredible journey in 'Actually I Can' shows us that laughter is not just the best medicine, but also a profound teacher. Her candid and humorous approach to life's challenges is both refreshing and inspiring. This is your go-to guide offering valuable lessons on resilience, gratitude, and the transformative power of joy." Nancy Lewis Hill, Confidence & Mindful Living Mentor

ACKNOWLEDGEMENTS

They say it takes a village, and in my case, it took a global community of incredibly supportive and amazing humans, spanning from my closest loved ones to millions on the web.

Here's a big shoutout to my favorite people in the world:

- My family, the superheroes who mastered the art of caring and made bed rest feel like a spa retreat. You turned medicine schedules into fun games and hospital rooms into comedy clubs. For all this and a million more acts of love and kindness, my heart overflows with gratitude.
- My friends, the extraordinary gang of meal deliverers and mood lifters. Thank you for turning my doorstep into a culinary hotspot and my phone into a hotline of laughter.
- My social media buddies, my digital lifeline. Thanks for virtually holding my hand, sending emojis and jokes that were often better than prescribed medicine, and making me smile wider than even my selfies could capture.
- My medical team, the rockstars in scrubs and masks. You not only saved my life but did it with style and grace.

To each one of you, I owe a slice of my journey. Without your unique contributions, my story would have been far less colorful and definitely not as laughter-filled. Here's to the power of community, love, and a whole lot of humor!

ACTUALLY, I CAN

INTRO

My cancer went viral . . . literally. The story of my journey reached hundreds of millions of people globally.

But this isn't a book about cancer. It's about joy. And laughter. And making up your own rules as you carve the life you want to lead.

I'm writing this book to show how someone at the top of her game can be suddenly struck with life-altering news, and intentionally choose the path of positivity and humor to overcome adversity and face an unfathomable challenge.

And inspire millions in the process!

I'm writing this book because courage is contagious. Optimism and inspiration spread. And humor makes everything easier.

Even when you have cancer. Scratch that. *Especially* when you have cancer—in my case, invasive lobular carcinoma, a form of breast cancer.

Interestingly, my breasts had been a point of focus well before my diagnosis. Back in college, I was awarded the title of "Best Breasts in the Dorm." Ah, the frivolity of youth.

Although a playful contest, that "honor" did impact me. Being known as the girl with the big breasts became a huge part of my identity.

Little did I know that years down the line my breasts would be at the center of another defining chapter of my life, albeit in a far more serious context.

I am going to let you in on a secret I've discovered—a secret you can use if you choose to approach adversity in an unconventional way, if you want to defy the expected and achieve what others may see as impossible, and if you want to use your own experiences with overcoming difficulties to impact and empower others.

But I wouldn't be writing this book if I hadn't begun a journey with breast cancer. I wouldn't have felt qualified.

Cancer changes things.

As an entrepreneur, wife, mother of a teenager, and daughter of loving parents who live close by, I recognized that this insidious disease goes beyond me. It has a profound impact on those closest to me: my family, my friends, even my employees and clients. What I didn't realize immediately is that the way I dealt with my circumstance could also significantly affect millions of others in a positive way.

From the moment I received my diagnosis, and through every step of my unexpected roller coaster of a journey, it would have been so easy to let my mind go to dark places. When you are presented with scary news, the path to despair is clearly laid out. It is obvious.

In fact, there are external and internal forces that obdurately and continuously push and pull you to follow the expected and well-trodden path.

Kübler-Ross Grief Model

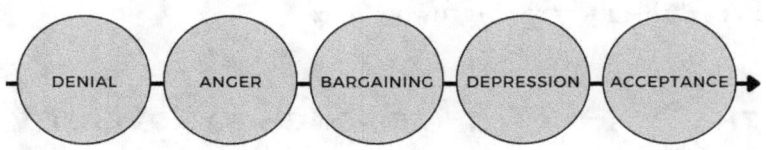

Originally created to describe the emotional stages of people facing terminal illness, the Kübler-Ross model has become more broadly applied as a framework for understanding grief in general.

I could have let this sorrow overwhelm me. And not one person would have criticized me for it. After all, I was facing the inevitability of having my breasts removed, as well as the very real possibility of a long journey filled with sickness and pain—while losing my hair to boot!

And, of course, at the beginning, I had no idea of the extent of my illness or if I would even survive. Who would blame me for being consumed with fear and depression?

But thankfully I saw the possibility of another route.

As far as I knew, this trail had never been blazed, but I felt deep inside that I could create a new pathway. I decided to venture into that uncharted territory and design my own roadmap.

In doing so, I found myself solidifying a personal philosophy

I had been unintentionally cultivating over the past couple of decades. By embracing this empowering and exciting mindset, I could meet my upcoming challenges with joyful anticipation, curiosity, and enthusiasm.

I am thrilled to reveal it to you here.

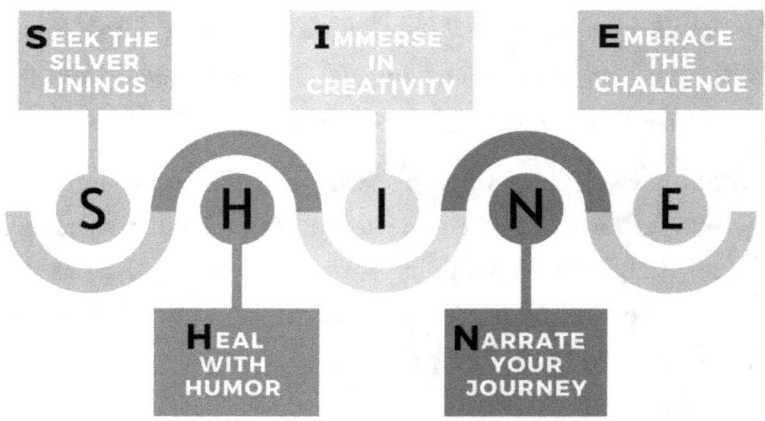

THE *Unexpected* APPROACH TO ADVERSITY

SEEK THE SILVER LININGS

IMMERSE IN CREATIVITY

EMBRACE THE CHALLENGE

S H I N E

HEAL WITH HUMOR

NARRATE YOUR JOURNEY

Seek the Silver Linings: Discovering Light in the Most Unexpected Places

 Conventional mindset: To feel grateful, focus on positive things more than negative things. You can't be grateful for negative things.

 Empowered response: *Actually, I can.*

Gratitude creates a positive feedback loop. The more we feel gratitude, the more we have to feel grateful for. The more we focus on what's good in our lives, the more our brain looks for things to smile about.

This is easy to understand when we are grateful for *positive* things. But grateful for *adversity*? Oh, yes. There is so much to be thankful for.

I pushed the boundaries of traditional positive psychology research and challenged the status quo around gratitude to prove that thankfulness isn't just reserved for rainbows and butterflies.

Heal with Humor: Finding the Funny

 Conventional mindset: There's nothing funny about cancer. To jest in the face of such adversity is inappropriate and futile. You can't laugh your way through this situation.

 Empowered response: *Actually, I can.*

During my cancer escapade, humor wasn't just a sidekick; it was my secret weapon, a superhero shield against overwhelm and anxiety.

Wrapping myself in the cape of humor, I found the power to unveil the hilarity in (almost) every situation, no matter how hard it was to find.

Laughter not only dialed down my apprehension and released those sweet stress-reducing endorphins, it also allowed me to bond deeply with others, turning presumed moments of despair into pockets of shared joy.

Science has my back on this one. Laughter is a bona fide health booster, with myriad benefits that range from enhancing immunity to easing pain. Spoiler alert: I've got cool studies to back that up!

Immerse in Creativity: Diving Into a Creative Outlet to Escape, Process, and Heal

 Conventional mindset: Challenges of this magnitude are all-consuming. You cannot simply avoid their shadows or find even a momentary escape.

 Empowered response: *Actually, I can.*

Diving deep into the world of creative outlets became my sanctuary. When I felt overwhelmed, I sought refuge in these havens of expression.

Creative outlets are more than just distractions. They're tools for healing, helping us process complex emotions, envision alternative narratives, and establish connections with deeper parts of ourselves that are better equipped to cope with our situation. These practices aren't about escaping reality; they are about reshaping our perceptions and gathering strength from within.

And having fun!

For me, creative expression functioned as a shelter during the stormiest nights.

Narrate Your Journey: Reframing and Rewriting Your Story

 Conventional mindset: Facts are immutable. They cannot be altered. You can't rewrite your story.

 Empowered response: *Actually, I can.*

Yes, there was one relentless fact that I couldn't change. I had cancer. But there's more to this story than that simple fact.

I believe we're not just characters in the tales of our lives, but also the authors. The words we whisper to ourselves shape our realities more often than we realize. These inner monologues have the power to uplift or undermine us.

By choosing the narrative, the language, and the tone in which I shared my journey, I wasn't just painting a picture for the world; I was sketching out the roadmap for my own psyche.

Through this book, you'll learn that you, too, wield the quill. Deploy this power, and you can write your own empowering stories.

Embrace the Challenge: Moving Past Acceptance and Enjoying the Journey

 Conventional mindset: While you can try to **accept** the idea of going through chemotherapy, it isn't something you can **embrace** or **welcome** as a cherished companion.

 Empowered response: *Actually, I can.*

The saying goes, "Life isn't about waiting for the storm to pass but learning to dance in the rain."

And dance I did. While it's natural to wish away difficult moments while waiting for the sun to come out, I chose to welcome the storm and revel in the raindrops.

Instead of seeking shelter and hiding away, I twirled in the tempest. Dancing in the rain meant discovering joy in places I hadn't looked before. I hope you can learn to uncover the same rhythm and embrace the downpours that make life's dance so beautifully provocative.

Why wait for a break in the clouds when there's an absolutely delicious puddle to jump in right now?

Start transforming your approach to adversity today. Download your own copy of The Unexpected Adversity Model graphic. Keep this handy tool as a guide for transforming challenges into opportunities. Get your copy here: www.actuallyicanbook.com

When you see how I approached my ordeal with positivity, humor, and excitement (believe it or not!), you'll understand how it's possible for you to face your own struggles in a different light.

During my cancer journey, I dove deep into narrating my experiences and sharing them in creative ways (which includes many of the elements of The Unexpected Approach to Adversity). Social media played an enormous role in keeping me grounded. It served as a creative outlet, a connection to the outside world, and a source for documenting my experiences, feelings, and clinical updates. In each chapter, I share the deeply personal, vulnerable, and often humorous posts that helped me generate millions of views and hundreds of thousands of followers along the way.

This book is a call to action for women everywhere. It's time to stop following the oft-prescribed, expected, and confining path that emphasizes victimhood, misery, and hopelessness, and blaze our own trails, write our own stories, and create our own powerful, authentic lives.

LET'S START WITH THE GOOD NEWS

Nika Stewart
January 7, 2020 · 🌐   •••

I feel like it's time to share what I've been going through for the past 4 weeks. I'll start with the good news...

I'm having a mastectomy.

(Yes! You can imagine how scary things seemed for that to be good news 🙂)

I'll also say that I am feeling not only physically great, but emotionally fine. Actually - strangely - I feel wonderful. (This may change in the next few days as we get closer to surgery, but for now...)

The hardest thing I've gone through in the past month is *waiting* (setting appointments, more tests, waiting for results, more tests) - with no answers and no clear path or schedule.

But now I seem to have a tentative schedule for surgery next week. So this week I'll be diving in deep to do as much work as I can. Luckily I have an amazing work team to care for our clients, and an amazing life team to take care of me 🥰

 223   524 Comments

I'll start with the good news . . .

I'm having a mastectomy.

I felt a giant rock in my chest as I pressed POST on this Facebook update. This was certainly not my usual content.

On the other hand, it was exactly like my usual content.

While social media is filled with airbrushed highlight reels and sporadic pleas for sympathy, I prefer my posts to be personal, open, and, most importantly, rooted in optimism.

And I've always believed that sharing our stories, especially during challenging times, creates a bond with our community. Our followers and connections become fellow travelers on our journey, sharing our tears and laughter, while offering their support.

I enjoy sharing posts infused with gratitude and authenticity.

My unexpected moments of joy as the parent of a teenager . . .

The weird excitement I find in mundane daily tasks . . .

Unusual ways to laugh at common business stressors . . .

My friends and followers were already accustomed to a cocktail of honesty mixed with a dash of sarcastic humor.

I wanted this post, although it discussed a heavier topic, to still carry my signature blend, a synthesis of gratitude, optimism, and truth.

But I was dropping a bomb.

So when I posted my big reveal, I had a feeling it would arouse a stronger-than-usual reaction.

What I didn't realize at the time, however, was that this was the starting gun—the spark that ignited my public journey. With this Facebook post, I embarked on an odyssey that would play out on the world's digital stage.

But this voyage had secretly begun six weeks earlier . . .

PAMPHLETS

November

One challenge I'm still trying to solve is that, as an adult, no one holds you accountable for doing the things that need to get done to be a productive, healthy, happy human.

As children, our lives are meticulously plotted out. It's like we're acting out parts in a play, where every scene is directed, every line whispered into our ears before we utter it. Our meals are prepared for us, our clothes are washed and laid out, our schedules are set. For a child, the world is a web of safety nets.

When you're a kid, other people guide you. Parents, guardians, and other adults make sure dental appointments are made, bedtimes are reasonably adhered to, and annual checkups are never missed. We float through days obliviously, taking for granted the myriad tasks silently managed for us. All the gears of our life are oiled and turned by hands other than our own.

But as the years roll on, that safety net thins, and the chorus of guiding voices grows quieter.

This happens gradually, and by the time adulthood emerges, we have been through a lot of rehearsals. We are now supposed to be prepared for the production of life.

But I am often still surprised to find myself on the stage with no script.

I am not only the actor but also the director, the producer, and perhaps most daunting—the *writer* of my own show.

Without a seasoned playwright scripting our moves or an experienced director prompting our next actions, it becomes alarmingly easy to skip scenes or omit essential lines.

Ignoring that annual doctor's appointment is a simple script change, so easy to do when there's no stage manager to cue you. It seems like a forgivable omission in the grand narrative. After all, the protagonist feels perfectly fine (in this act, anyway).

As a responsible adult, I try to create ways to hold myself accountable for the important tasks. For example, I set reminders. Then my calendar sends me messages when it's time to do something.

But I never had to set a reminder to schedule my annual mammogram, because the women's health center sets next year's appointment before I leave each visit. At least that's one adulting responsibility I can forgo.

Each year, a few weeks before my appointment, I get a note—sent by some other responsible adult or by an automated system. I love that this is taken care of for me.

I also appreciate that at my women's health center, the mammogram and ultrasound (necessitated by my dense breast tissue which makes accurate findings difficult with just the mammogram alone) are performed in the same facility at the same appointment, *and* the doctor looks at the readouts and gives me results before I leave. There is no waiting and worrying.

"All good. See you next year!" the doctor says each time as I leave.

But this particular year, instead of getting a reminder for an upcoming appointment, I received a letter telling me the center had closed.

The script I followed for years had just been thrown in the trash.

This meant going back to adulting myself for this task, holding myself accountable for scheduling these annual mammogram appointments.

Since scheduling a mammogram at a new facility required gathering all my past information and results, I procrastinated. Without my familiar script, I felt overwhelmed with choices and responsibilities. And life. Many other more immediate productions called for my performance. And honestly, the mammogram was just a minor role, right?

After all, the protagonist felt perfectly fine.

Instead of receiving my mammogram twelve months after my last one, my appointment came eighteen months later.

No big deal. Because I don't get bad results.

This new facility was nothing like the center I had gone to for a decade. They didn't have the equipment to perform ultrasounds. And they didn't read your results the day of your appointment. You simply took your top off, got a quick mammo, and said goodbye. Wham-bam-scan-you-ma'am!

"We'll call you if there is anything concerning," they said as I left.

And then they did.

They called and told me to have an ultrasound because they'd found spots they wanted to look at.

No surprise here. I *always* need to have an ultrasound because—like I said—my breasts are quite dense, and the ultrasound is the only way the doctor can see more clearly that there is nothing to worry about.

I set the appointment for the ultrasound at another new facility. Fortunately, in that place they read the results right away, and shared them with you before you left. So, after the tests were completed, I got dressed and went into the little room where you sit in a comfortable chair and wait for a doctor to come in and say, "All good. See you next year!"

But when I looked up, I saw not one, but *two* people walking into my room. And they were carrying pamphlets.

GROUND ZERO—THE DEFINING MOMENT

Time froze.

It's difficult to recall the exact thoughts I had and the feelings that coursed through my body when I saw those ominous pamphlets in their hands. But I remember immediately knowing this was a pivotal moment.

I can cite this moment as Ground Zero—the real start to my journey through diagnosis, treatment, and recovery. My cancer story began the moment I looked up and saw these women with pamphlets.

The pamphlets weren't the only red flag. It was also peculiar to see two people come into the room. It felt fishy.

I wonder why they have two people come into the room when there is bad news to share. Seriously, how many healthcare professionals does it take to change a light—I mean, break bad news to a patient? I get it, though; I wouldn't want to be tasked with breaking this kind of bad news alone.

Before the women sat down next to me, I knew I was not walking out of the room unscathed. Without reading the pamphlets, I had a good idea of what they indicated.

They didn't give me a diagnosis at this meeting. I was only here to learn, they told me, whether or not I should take another test to clarify the results of my ultrasound. Of course, I need not worry, I assured myself, as I knew that ultrasounds often lead to further testing. Many women have screenings that show something suspicious, necessitating additional analysis, but turn out to be perfectly fine in the end.

Yet, I somehow knew this was different. The demeanor of the women, the heaviness of the air in the room, and the brandishing of those telltale pamphlets all told me my life was about to be derailed.

I had no idea of the path I would be taking, but I instinctively knew I would be at least dipping my toe into a world I had been blissfully shielded from. After a decade of "See you next year," I was now getting a "Something looks suspicious."

Nothing was definite. "Suspicious" doesn't mean cancerous. It just means further probing needs to be done. I was being told I should have another test.

Needle biopsies were recommended. One of the women—the doctor who had looked at the ultrasound results—said two areas looked unusual: one spot on my breast and a node under my arm.

That's when I realized I needed to explain things. It was time to clear up this misunderstanding.

My first response was to tell her that this additional step was completely unnecessary.

"My breasts are very dense," I told her.

I "patient-splained" to this medical professional that it is difficult to know what you are seeing when the breast is dense.

"My past doctor sees these unusual looking spots every year, and they turn out to be nothing."

I half expected her to say, "Oh! Okay, thanks for letting me know. All good. See you next year!"

But she calmly and sympathetically told me she had looked at my films from the past decade, and these suspicious spots were indeed *new*.

I listened quietly as the other woman explained the biopsy procedure to me. A technician would use a special needle to extract cells from my breast and under my arm.

I wished that my husband was there. I wanted emotional support.

I was glad my husband wasn't there. I didn't want to be worrying about anyone else's feelings.

The nurse handed me the pamphlets. They detailed what to expect, how to prepare, and what the results might show.

I wished that my husband was there. I needed him to tell me there was no reason to worry.

I was glad my husband wasn't there. It was much easier learning what my next step would be without someone else interrupting with their own concerns and questions.

The doctor handed me a prescription and told me to schedule the biopsy procedure as soon as possible.

I wished that my husband was there. I could be strong if he was holding my hand.

I remember experiencing a powerful and dizzying blend of emotions, with surprise, fear, and confusion leading the pack.

But now I want to share another feeling I had . . .

Excitement.

Huh?

I realize you probably think I am insane. Only a crazy person would feel excitement when presented with a terrifying, potentially catastrophic possibility.

But this is the start of my choosing the path of positivity.

It happened so quickly that I didn't notice the thought process at the time.

While I had always embraced this glass-half-full philosophy—focus on the bright side, choose positivity—I never really had the opportunity to practice it in a significant way. Until this point, my primary challenges were common, everyday problems we all face—relationship struggles, business obstacles, home project failures. And while they consumed me at the time—they all paled in comparison to this behemoth.

Sure, anyone can look at the bright side when dealing with a challenge at work, but how many can carry this optimism through when faced with a potentially *life-threatening* diagnosis? Could I really practice what I preach?

I didn't know for sure . . . yet. But after years of intentionally looking for silver linings, feeling gratitude, and searching for lessons embedded in difficult situations, I instinctively saw the opportunity for adventure.

Adventure?

Sure! This was a new experience. My mind would be opened. I'd learn new things. I could document the encounter and have new stories to tell.

Of course, there might be physical pain and emotional anxiety, but I could also look at this unique experience with wonder and curiosity. I could jump in with enthusiasm. I could choose to feel joy.

If you are dubiously squinting your eyes, thinking that is ludicrous, then my goal in this book is to convince you otherwise.

When I reflect on how I was able to get through these years with a positive attitude, I can attribute it to making deliberate, intentional choices instead of following a pre-written script.

And I had some incredible opportunities to make choices as new characters entered my story.

I'm looking forward to introducing you to an ironic "legend" in the biopsy world, a bumbling country doctor who wields power over life and death at the bottom of a stack of papers in his fax machine, and the dreaded "Red Devil" (even worse than the name implies!).

CHOOSING A DIFFERENT LENS

In life's stormy moments, there's always a choice: dwell on the fear, the inconvenience, the disappointment, or embrace the unique beauty those moments can offer.

This is true even outside the context of a traumatic or life-altering event. In fact, you likely had several opportunities this very week to choose how you would feel and react to negative situations. You probably don't have to think too far back to remember when someone cut you off on the highway. You had a choice. React angrily and let the situation escalate until you are seen on the next episode of "Road Rage Goes Awry," or simply chuckle at the blatant rudeness of some of our fellow humans and look forward to sharing the incident with your spouse.

The point is that it is up to you. This is just as true with minor daily aggravations as it is with more serious events with harsher consequences.

> *"Each player must accept the cards life deals him or her; but once they are in hand, he or she alone must decide how to play the cards in order to win the game."*
> *– Voltaire*

My husband and I often reinforced this idea with my daughter. For example, when she was troubled by the persistently crabby demeanor and ongoing insensitive comments made by her fifth-grade art teacher, we turned it into a game. She would receive one point for every minor remark and three points for more egregious behavior, which could then be redeemed at the end of the year for a prize. She enjoyed the game so much that it got to a point where, instead of dreading the class and obnoxious teacher, she actually looked forward to accumulating points. What a difference perspective makes!

Roommate Gone Wrong

My first memory of choosing positivity over despair.

I felt like the rug had been pulled out from under me.

In my second year of college, I was excited to move back into the dorm I had loved so much during freshman year. And the best part? I had won the "room lottery." My name was picked first from a large list, and I got to choose my favorite room in the dorm to live in for the year.

Unfortunately, a mix-up meant three freshmen got the large, open, corner room. By the time I realized the blunder, the only room left was the one no one wanted—a cubbyhole disguised as a dorm room with perfectly engineered dimensions that allowed two people of less-than-average mass who, only by holding in their tummies, could pass by one another with only moderate body contact.

No, there really wasn't room for more than one person in this tiny prison cell; nonetheless, two of us would share the space.

And then I met my roommate, Tammy.

We had different backgrounds and interests, and I was looking forward to expanding my mind, learning more about her and her passions, and becoming friendly with someone I would likely have never otherwise met.

My enthusiasm quickly faded. Not only did I feel cramped in my space, but my roomie was not as pleasant as I had hoped.

Oh, she wasn't outwardly nasty. But she seemed to have no respect for me or my things.

Like my phone, for example.

Quick history lesson: There was a time in the distant past when the idea of walking around with a personal phone was only discussed in the most outlandish science fiction novels. When I was in college, our only options for telecommunication were to use the dorm payphone (like you see in prison movies) or to install a costly physical phone into the wall of our room. These "land lines" came with burdensome monthly fees, plus additional charges for every phone call.

Although I was a typical broke college student, I decided having my own phone was a priority, so I adjusted my budget to afford this luxury.

The account was in my name, and I paid the bills. Tammy enjoyed using "our" phone and relaxing on loud, lengthy calls with her friends; but when it was time to pay the bill, she was flat out of cash.

On the food front, she felt no remorse availing herself of my snacks. I had no problem with sharing, but she rarely bought anything. Thankfully, she was conscientious and considerate enough to often "replace" what she had taken. For example, she would eat one of my custom-baked, gourmet, bakery specials that I decided to splurge on, and then replace it with a two-day-old leftover blueberry muffin from Mike's QuikMart.

Or maybe those dried black dots were raisins? (It's a strong possibility—still awaiting lab results.) In any case, the mature muffins packed a surprising crunch. I don't know this from eating them. Her loud chewing would often wake me in the early morning.

Showering was a rare occurrence for her. It didn't seem a priority. So our teeny dorm-cave smelled bad. She didn't notice or care. I did.

I know I've made my point, yet I continue.

I constantly worried about disturbing her since our room was so small. When she was sleeping, I dressed in the dark. I'd sneak around as quietly as I could.

She, on the other hand, acted like there was no one else in the room. When she woke in the morning—even if I was still asleep, she turned on the light. She munched noisily on her stale muffins. She blew her hair. She talked on "our" phone, unencumbered by the financial burden typically associated with frequent, leisurely, long-distance calls.

And then there was her preaching. Oh, the preaching. Disturbed by my lack of affiliation with her particular religious sect, she was besieged with the overwhelming compulsion to continuously educate me about the urgency of my acceptance of her sacred beliefs.

And as appealing as it was to join a group where a lack of self-awareness and moral compass was apparently acceptable—and possibly encouraged or mandated—I managed to resist.

The first few weeks of that year became a struggle. Faced with the prospect of an agonizing, lonely year, with an inconsiderate, ill-hygiened, crunchy-muffin-eating, preachy, low-key bully as an almost constant companion, it was clear my year would be filled with anxiety, frustration, conflict, and unhappiness.

Not acceptable. I had to find another way to navigate this situation.

So I found the perfect solution.

I hired a hitman.

Only kidding. Obviously, I couldn't afford an assassin. All my disposable income was spent supporting her sophisticated confectionary habit and paying for her long-distance phone calls.

The only solution was to choose a different focus.

When we are presented with circumstances over which we have little to no control, we can still control our thoughts and our feelings. I chose wonder and amusement.

As I talked about my roommate's shenanigans with friends, I realized how hysterical it was. She really did seem like a caricature of a nightmare roommate. I could choose to look at my situation as a fun opportunity.

Just as I later created a point system with my daughter to deal with her bossy art teacher, I turned this into a game as well.

I began to make notes about her infractions and then share these events with friends. I didn't earn any points, but they were entertaining stories. My friends wondered how far she would actually go and waited to hear what shocking thing she did next.

I stayed over in friends' rooms and apartments many nights and formed lots of close relationships.

I felt motivated to decorate our room with geometric wall hangings and colorful accessories, so I could create a space that felt cheerful. If our door was left open (as it so often was, so I could air out the stuffy smell), everyone who walked by did a double take and stopped, staring in awe at our cute little cubicle. Our room became the talk of the dorm, and others asked me to add fun touches to their spaces. This ignited my love for creative interior design.

Rooming with someone I didn't want to live with for nine months wasn't going to change. But I could change my attitude and mindset. I chose joy, and it turned out to be an excellent college year. Looking back on how much I gained during that time, I find myself grateful for the experience.

My repulsion for raisins in baked goods, however, persists to this day.

Are you ready to rewrite your narrative? Download our Story Shift workbook, filled with exercises to help you transform your perspective and your experience.
www.actuallyicanbook.com

TOO BUSY FOR YOUR CANCER

If you think this next chapter is my indictment of the healthcare industry, you would be partially correct. While my journey afforded me the opportunity to meet true medical heroes, I also experienced the burden of a convoluted bureaucracy that not only caused endless frustration, but also significantly impeded my care.

I walked out of the small room with pamphlets in my hand and scheduled a biopsy procedure.

Wait. That's not entirely true.

If you've ever attempted to set an appointment for any medical procedure, you know that is an oversimplification.

I did not just pick up the phone to schedule a biopsy. You wouldn't expect someone who is worried about cancer to be able to quickly and easily set an appointment, do you? Despite the urgency of my situation, there were hoops I needed to jump through to schedule my test.

I was directed to an office for a scheduling consultation. The scheduler looked for the next available appointment. She put my name in for the end of the week, then printed out what seemed like reams of paper.

I had to read and sign many forms guaranteeing that I would pay for the procedure if my insurance didn't cover it.

Although I was fairly confident my insurance would allow a biopsy (this is an important, necessary procedure, right?), I asked what the cost was. If I was going to sign a legal document stating that I would accept financial responsibility, I should know the amount I might be paying. Could I even afford it? Or would I have to mortgage my house to cover this test?

The woman couldn't tell me.

"Probably a few thousand dollars," she casually chirped.

I signed all the papers, assuming this was too important a procedure to worry about money.

Then she told me that even though the appointment was set, it was dependent on the insurance company approving it.

But hadn't I just signed papers saying I would take care of the billing if the insurance company didn't approve it?

The health center still needed approval from my insurance.

And I had only three days to get it. The clock was ticking.

To make the situation more fun, the codes wouldn't even be sent to the insurance company until my primary care doctor signed off on the procedure.

Wait—what? Why was my primary care doctor involved? He didn't care for my breasts (although I did notice an occasional stare)!

But the center that performed my mammogram required a prescription, and since I had gotten one automatically every year from my primary care doctor, that's who I listed on my original paperwork. Now his name was on my entire case as the approving doctor.

Dr. M—the local GP I had seen several times for occasional sore throats and annual flu shots—was now, unfortunately and unintentionally, the captain of my healthcare team for the cancer diagnosis, and was required to approve all procedures related to the initial mammogram. Nothing would move forward until he signed off on the next steps.

They faxed the request. As soon as I got home, I called his office to confirm that he would send in the paperwork. The insurance company could not approve the procedure until they got his signature, and we only had three days. I was assured that he would do it as soon as possible.

He didn't.

The biopsy date was nearing quickly. We waited for the doctor's approval.

I called the next day and was told that the doctor was a very busy man. He received a lot of fax papers. He certainly couldn't get to everything right away.

I explained the situation to the woman on the phone. I now had only two days to get the request signed and sent to the insurance company so they could approve the procedure. Unfortunately, my urgency was neither contagious nor appreciated.

In fact, she seemed annoyed.

Toward the end of the day, I still hadn't heard from the doctor or the insurance company. My next phone call to the doctor was answered by a younger-sounding girl who knew nothing about my situation. She said she would ask Dr. M and call me back.

When I still hadn't gotten a phone call an hour later, I called the doctor's office and listened to a recorded message telling me the office was closed for the day.

I felt like there were bombs exploding inside me. My entire body boiled with fury, but I had no outlet for release. I wanted to scream at the doctor and the uncaring people in his office. I wanted to tell someone at the insurance company that the entire system needed to be changed. How could I not have a cancer test approved? Why did I have to get a signature from someone who wasn't connected in any way to my breasts? To someone who was not a cancer specialist? Why was I forced to wait without information during a time when I was terrified of a grim diagnosis?

I felt neglected and ignored when I should have been prioritized.

After taking a few (a hundred) deep breaths, I reminded myself that, despite these external hiccups, I held a certain control over the events.

This was so early in the journey that I had no idea how much of that control I'd need to harness. Looking back, it seems like this was the first big test of my spirit.

Yes, although the system is flawed and maddeningly bureaucratic, "actually, I can" take charge of my reactions.

So, instead of letting the frustration consume me, I decided to channel that energy. I reached out to a few close friends and invited them to go out to dinner.

As we waited for our meal to arrive, I shared the insanity of the last few days.

Their support was unwavering. They echoed my frustrations, shared similar stories, and offered words of comfort.

One of my buddies even offered to ring up the doc's office for me. Bless her heart! And when she shared the—let's say—"passionately crafted" script of what she'd say to him? I nearly fell out of the booth laughing.

I swear, the pure, unfiltered, sassy support of my friends could cure any ailment. They reminded me that I wasn't going to let the negligence of one doctor define my entire experience.

After many more calls the next day begging for him to sign my paper, he finally sent the approval—just in time for my scheduled biopsy procedure. The form then went to my insurance company, who told me that this biopsy center was not covered by my plan, and I'd have to choose a different place.

Of course, it was now too late to find a new place and schedule something for the next day. My procedure was canceled.

CHOOSE HAPPY?

How is it possible to feel joy when you are planning for surgery to remove your breasts?

How can you laugh and be happy when you are waiting for scan results that will tell you if your cancer has spread to other parts of your body?

How can you be silly and make others smile when you are watching your hair and eyelashes fall out?

How?

The answer is simple, yet profound: You choose to.

I don't get to choose what is thrown at me, what other people do or say, how the stock market is doing, whether it rains or shines . . .

. . . *but I am 100% responsible for my thoughts about those circumstances.* And my thoughts—what I decide to focus on—determine how I feel.

Events don't cause feelings. Our thoughts about those events do.

Consider this scenario. You're walking with a friend when a stranger approaches, asking for aid. Your heart might swell with sympathy, while your friend feels a pinch of annoyance.

Same situation, different reactions.

Why?

Because of the stories you both form in your minds about that moment.

Your narrative might be woven with threads of compassion, pondering the challenges the stranger faces.

Your friend, meanwhile, might be stitching a tale of inconvenience and interruption.

We each have the power to spin our own yarns, changing the patterns as we see fit.

However, a gentle reminder: while we possess the freedom to interpret our situations, this doesn't mean every interpretation should radiate sunshine. Some situations beg for a richer palette of emotions to inspire action or urgency.

Some circumstances require feelings to move us, motivate us, galvanize us to take actions that produce results we want.

Perhaps sadness propels you into lending a hand, while anger might ignite a passion to combat the inherent inequalities around us.

True, my narratives often hum with positivity.

But when my doctor turned a blind eye, I needed to act. I had to find a team of medical experts who would support me.

So I chose thoughts and feelings that led to quick action. This was not a circumstance that warranted patience.

Annoyance. Anger. Anxiety. These were the feelings I needed. And boy did I embrace them!

They provoked me into doing more research. They motivated me to investigate other options. My anger pushed me to keep calling until I found a facility that would see me. I harnessed the emotions required to achieve the results I so desperately needed.

And thank goodness I did. As it turned out, the cancer had spread, so waiting even a few more weeks could have been devastating.

So, while my tale might champion positivity, it also reminds us that life requires a gamut of emotions to produce the results needed for each circumstance.

Wanna master your emotions? You can transform your trials into triumphs by getting your own copy of the SHINE Emotional Mastery Playbook at www.actuallyicanbook.com

Even my social media posts at the time hinted at a change coming and my growing frustration.

Nika Stewart ✓
December 5, 2019 · 🌐

Trying to breathe into this extremely frustrating, anger-inducing day. As much as I want to scream and pull my hair out of my head (and at the same time, crawl under my covers and cry), I also totally appreciate that I've designed my life and my business for this exact purpose: To have the flexibility to take care of the unexpected, without sacrificing other priorities.

So I am grateful. And I am acutely pissed off at a lot of people (and the entire health care system).

That day, I drove around the county, hopping from one medical center to the next, picking up records and dropping them off, begging for a swift biopsy appointment. Amidst the mounting frustration, I also felt overwhelming gratitude. I was thankful for the liberty to do this. My past self had designed my business and life with this very freedom in mind—freedom to shift gears and focus on what truly mattered. And here I was, living it.

While I had always been a frequent content poster, little did I know that my social media presence would turn out to be my life-saving tie to the outside world, a needed source to generate support throughout my ordeal, a way to cultivate meaningful friendships, and a vehicle that would help me inspire millions of people from around the world.

FLYING BABY ELEPHANT

In the wake of my suddenly axed biopsy appointment, the days that followed morphed into an exhaustive game of phone-tag and circuitous drives around town. I felt caught in a maddening scavenger hunt, collecting records from one place, only to drop them off at another.

The persistently peppy and repetitive on-hold music during my countless calls to the insurance company and healthcare facilities, mixed with the unrelenting maze of automated responses, only heightened my agitation.

Every delay felt like an eternity, and the days dragged on.

You might think for something as critical as a cancer test, the system would move with urgency. But this wasn't the case at all. It seemed like the medical industry itself was plotting against me.

An unwritten script suggested I should accept this snail-paced process and allow things to move on their typical timeline.

But heck, this was my life we were talking about! Patience may be a virtue, but this wasn't the time for it.

After what felt like an endless loop of frustration, I finally wrestled down an appointment. But it was still a week away—another week of nerve-wracking waiting.

My husband and I tried not to worry.

Have you ever tried not to worry? It's like trying not to think of a flying baby elephant. Don't think of it! Don't!

SNAP! A BIOPSY BALLET

Setting: A modern-day medical center, brightly lit.

Center stage is a high-tech bed, and beside it, a large screen showing real-time images of the inside of a body. The backdrop morphs into a futuristic, sci-fi setting.

The leading lady, robed and poised, steps in stage right, absorbing the environment, a mix of wonder and anxiety in her eyes.

~~~

Finally, the day of the long-awaited biopsy is upon me.

I change into the flimsy robe and go into an office to be prepped. I'm told that Donna is going to administer my biopsy, and oh boy, am I lucky it's her!

As they wheel me into what looks like a futuristic movie set, it seems everyone is a member of the Donna Fan Club.

"Oh, Donna's on your case? Lucky you."

"Donna? A biopsy rockstar."

I'm lying there thinking, "Wow, did I win the biopsy lottery or what?"

Then, in walks Donna—surprisingly, without a cape. She points out this nifty monitor where I can watch the behind-the-scenes action inside my own body. Cool, right?

So, there I am, with a starring role in the biopsy biopic directed by a true legend, complete with a funky soundtrack every time they take a sample.

Snap! Into the sterile container it goes, to be studied later by some co-star in the lab.

We finish the episode featuring my breasts and transition to the lymph node scene. I get to watch Donna play a tricky game of "Catch the Node" and, spoiler alert, the node is playing hard to get. Each time the needle gets close, it's like the node yells, "Psych!" and dodges away.

All the while, I'm gritting my teeth in pain, mentally sending Donna vibes like, "Come on, girl, fifth time's the charm!" Thankfully, I am blessed to have the cream of the biopsy crop fishing for my elusive node.

Finally, I have to turn my head from the screen and close my eyes, thinking maybe the node is shy and doesn't like me watching.

After what feels like a particularly dramatic dance sequence between the needle and the node, I hear that satisfying snap.

And just like that, the thrilling Biopsy Ballet episode is concluded.

I get dressed and a nurse hands me my parting gifts—a few fashionable pink ice packs. Who says invasive medical procedures can't be stylish?

POST NEEDLE GUNSLINGER

After my biopsy dance, I played the leading role in yet another thrilling installment of The Waiting Game.

I went back to my regularly scheduled life as mom, wife, business owner . . . because my biopsy results would take three to five days to arrive at their destination.

And guess where they were headed!

No, not to me.

And not to some renowned cancer guru who could explain the results to me.

No, they were taking a scenic route to my primary care doc— you know, the very one who had a borderline criminally negligent aversion to signing my original test papers on time.

Having some foresight about his extremely busy schedule and inclination to downplay the importance of timely communication, I called his office to give him the heads-up before jumping in the car to take my daughter for a hair appointment.

"Please let the doctor know that some vital info about my health will arrive in his inbox in a few days. Can you have him call to give me the results *as soon as they come in?*"

When my daughter Ellie and I walked into the salon, I put

my worries on pause and just soaked in her excitement about getting a new hairstyle.

But the shrill ring of my phone shattered my momentary peace. Recognizing the doctor's number, I quickly zipped up my jacket and stepped outside to take the call.

It was the doctor himself, taking time out of his busy schedule to educate me on proper protocol.

I paced the length of the parking lot, shivering in the winter air, as I restated my request to the doctor. "The results of my biopsy will come to you in a few days, so please call me immediately to share the results."

His response?

A heartwarming, "You don't think I'll actually share the news over the phone, do you?"

I watched my breath form worrying white clouds in the cold as I said, "Why yes, Doc, I was expecting that exact thing."

But no, apparently this was "bad medicine" in his book. He would not share any results over the phone.

Instead, he said, when the results came in, I could schedule an appointment to discuss my fate in person.

I'll admit it. I flipped my lid.

Buzzing with outrage, but trying to keep my voice under control since I was standing in a public area, I gritted my teeth and said, "You will have the answer in your hand, saying if I have cancer or not, but you won't tell me?"

He tried to soothe my ruffled feathers, saying they often had same-day appointments available, so I wouldn't have to wait too long.

And here's the kicker—if he was booked solid, I could have an appointment with one of his trusty sidekicks to break the news. Maybe even the same sidekick who hinted that quickly signing off on my test was too Herculean a task for their office.

The sensation of powerlessness was sharp. Control over my own narrative was slipping right through my fingers.

It felt like my doctor had taken on the role of author, drafting me into his own suspense novel. He held the pen, decided the twists, and reveled in the cliffhangers. I was a puppet in a tale of tension and uncertainty.

And the puppeteer pulling my strings seemed so detached, almost aloof, happy to keep me dangling over the abyss of uncertainty.

At my wits' end, I hit him with an ultimatum. Either he shared the results over the phone as soon as they were available, or he could send those results to another doctor, so he or she could share the news with me.

The chasm of silence after my demand was palpable.

My breaths grew quick and shallow, not just from the cold,

but from the rising tide of emotions threatening to spill over. It was as if we were two gunslingers in an old Western show-down, eyes locked, waiting for the other to flinch.

This was more than just about hearing results; it was about reclaiming a semblance of control in a world that had turned topsy-turvy.

He agreed to send my results to someone else. But—oh, actually, he was leaving to sip piña coladas on vacation for the next week, so some other brave soul in his office would take care of it for me.

By the time the bizarre conversation ended, with his casual mention of a tropical getaway and the delegated responsibility, I could tell my face was completely flushed, and not just from the biting wind.

I stood in the chilly parking lot, my heart pounding from the gravity of our conversation.

Then, with a heavy sigh, I re-entered the warmth of the salon. I stowed away my anger, switched gears, and put on my "mom" face. Watching my daughter's transformation and chatting with her about her new look was a sweet, grounding distraction.

And yet, amidst the hum of hairdryers and chit-chat, the weight of that phone call lingered, reminding me of the ever-present duality of our journeys. We get to write so much of our own story, but there are some chapters we just can't control.

What we *always* have command over, however, is how we roll with those unpredictable pages.

A few suspense-filled days later, I surprisingly got a call. It wasn't the doc. It wasn't his sidekick. It was an admin in the office. She said she had my results, and asked who she should forward them to.

Without thinking, I said, "Email them to me."

Then I held my breath.

Seems she didn't get the memo about "bad medicine," so she happily obliged.

JUST A HAIRCUT

Picture this. My husband, Rob, and I, huddled over a laptop on the side chair in our bedroom, about to unveil the secret contents from an email containing my long-awaited test results.

I don't know what made me think I could just look at the results and understand them. Last I checked, neither my husband nor I were rocking a stethoscope. (We had just finished rewatching a full season of *House*, but that probably didn't fully qualify us for accurately interpreting a radiological diagnosis.) The jumble of medical jargon staring back at us was as clear as mud.

I saw the words "carcinoma" and "in situ."

Naturally, Dr. Google came to the rescue. I assume all the best medical schools across the country advocate for checking the web to confirm and interpret a medical diagnosis.

After a few clicks and scrolls, I learned that while carcinoma did indeed mean cancer, when you added "in situ," it actually . . . wasn't quite cancer?

I found this on Google:

"Lobular carcinoma in situ (LCIS) isn't cancer. But being diagnosed with LCIS indicates that you have an increased risk of developing breast cancer."

Rob immediately released his tension as he breathed a loud sigh of relief.

Another search revealed:

"Sometimes if LCIS is found using a needle biopsy, the doctor might recommend that it be removed completely."

Our amateur detective skills led us to believe we might be dealing with a tiny blip on the radar. A nuisance, for sure, but not the end of the world.

To get more information, I reached out to the biopsy center. I got in touch with Donna, the renowned expert who'd played Beethoven on my underarm. I assumed she could explain what I didn't understand.

I shared the results with her, and she asked me what size the carcinoma was.

I looked at the paper and saw that the spot labeled carcinoma was .1m—a tenth of a millimeter. And no cancer was found in the nodes.

"Isn't that really small?" I asked her.

Donna agreed that it was indeed a tiny dot, and I was lucky. But she advised that when it came time to decide on how to treat it, I should go for the maximum.

"Don't just settle for a small procedure. Be the most aggressive you can."

That felt strange to me, but I couldn't put my finger on why. I was just so happy to hear this was only a minor hiccup that I blissfully moved on.

More phone calls flew. I called my mom and shared my results. She got her doctor on the line, who echoed the same tune—it was just a common, run-of-the-mill kind of issue. I would probably have a lumpectomy—an operation in which a lump is removed from the breast. No biggie.

The quirky analogy he offered?

"It'll be like a haircut."

I assume this was meant to put my mind at ease. The procedure I might face would be so simple and quick that I could compare it to a visit at the salon.

As if snipping split ends compared to snipping . . . well, let's not go there.

Oddly, this "haircut" comparison seemed to be the hot phrase among the medical brotherhood. I heard it several times that first week. And yes, every single doctor echoing this sentiment was of the XY chromosome variety. Go figure.

It did manage to take the edge off, though.

So here I was, facing what seemed to be a speed bump. A slight detour in my otherwise jam-packed schedule. A thing to be checked off my to-do list. After all, it was "just like a haircut." I reasoned I could probably have the procedure in the morning, stop by the salon for a mani-pedi on my way home as a reward, and still have time for a few client calls.

But let me tell you—my "haircut" had a heck of a twist ending. I ended up more like Sinead O'Connor than Farrah Fawcett.

BLISSFULLY IGNORANT

It's amazing how mistaken and incompetent some medical professionals were at the onset of my journey. But being blissfully ignorant lulled me into a false sense of safety, and looking back, I am grateful for that. I believe it was a blessing.

Instead of colliding head on with a Mac Truck, I was grazed by a tiny compact car, and I could absorb and digest that bit of scary news before I was smacked by another. And another. And another.

How Rob got me to do a full day of work… one tiny step at a time:

This morning felt tough. I was in some pain and could not get comfortable. All I wanted to do was lay in bed and whine. 😊

So my husband made me get up and get dressed. Damn him!

He helped me put on socks and a new shirt, even though I knew it was ridiculous. Obviously I was just going to get right back into bed. Then when I was all dressed, he said... "Okay, let's go downstairs!" WHAT? I humored him, but moaned all the way down the stairs.

Then he set me up in a comfortable chair with my laptop, coffee, and some breakfast. I sat for a while and whined some more.

And then...

I wrote a month's worth of post templates for SHINE 365!

My husband is my hero.

THE WAR KITCHEN

The first few days after receiving my diagnosis were like being in a war room.

Actually, that's ridiculous. I have no idea what a war room is like.

To be honest, I don't even know what a war room actually is. But when I cleared off all the counters and started frantically making phone calls, taking pages of notes, pinning dozens of papers onto a board, and creating bulging files, Rob called this area of our kitchen The War Room.

I had never dealt with cancer before. My knowledge on the topic was, at this point, in its infancy. Like most people who have not had cancer touch their lives personally, I only had a vague idea of what cancer is, what it does to the body, and what treatments are available. I needed guidance. But where does one even begin? How does someone even know where to look or whom to ask for guidance?

Was there a guru specializing in my diagnosis? A hotline I could call for answers? Where was the conductor to orchestrate this weird ballet? Who was going to help me to understand and manage what was happening?

I needed a director, but I didn't even have a script.

So many questions, each echoing louder than the last.

What. On. Earth. Do. I. Do?

With an air of grim determination, I reached for the first lifeline I could think of—my insurance company. Surely, they'd have a compass, a directory of knights in white lab coats, right?

They dispatched a list of doctors. Finally—a starting point. With every ounce of optimism and hope we could muster, Rob and I started dialing.

We became a call center. Rob dialed the first number on the list, and I picked up my phone to dial the next.

I paced around the counter as I waited for someone to pick up, listening to Rob ask about appointments and if our insurance would be accepted.

With every failed attempt, we crossed someone off the list and dialed the next doctor, hoping this one would give us the answer we needed.

We learned that many of the doctors on our insurance company's list would not actually accept our insurance. Others didn't even answer the phone. We left message after message and continued to call every number until we exhausted the list. As some providers began calling back, we were both juggling multiple phone calls at a time, trying to identify someone who could give us answers and create a roadmap for us to follow.

Despite the frenzy of our calls, however, I felt like we were wading through quicksand.

Okay, like the War Room reference, I also have no experience with quicksand. But every step, every call, felt laden, sluggish.

Were we communicating in slow motion, or had we landed in an alternate universe where time meandered at a more leisurely pace? The sense of urgency I felt seemed lost on the rest of the world.

"Please forward us your files. Once they're scrutinized by the doctor—who's probably sipping tea in another dimension, given the pace we're going—he'll let us know if you're a good candidate, and if so, we'll eventually pencil in an appointment for a tête-à-tête."

"Want your files? Sure. Draft a request, maybe pen a sonnet while you're at it, and perhaps, in about two eons . . . I mean, business days, someone might grace you with a response."

"Our next slot? Let me check. Ah! How does six weeks sound? Around the time when winter turns to spring. The garden in the front of our office will have flowers to greet you by then."

Six weeks?

My internal scream could've shattered glass. This wasn't a reservation for a trendy brunch spot. This was cancer! Didn't that demand immediate action? I didn't need an appointment in the distant future; I needed it yesterday. Urgency raced through my veins, but my pleas for action were met with apathy and indifference.

I felt helpless. There I was, a woman who prided herself on an exceptional ability to get things done efficiently, now lost in a labyrinth of bureaucracy and seemingly endless paperwork.

The kitchen counter had become the unwitting host to a sprawling city of medical files, dwarfed only by the rapidly depleting stack of sticky notes, each scrawled with cryptic messages and reminders.

My car was now doubling as a cross-state courier vehicle, so familiar with medical center parking lots and doctors' offices that I half expected it to drive itself there.

Each day I spent hours in the kitchen, phone pressed to my ear, waiting for that infuriating elevator music signaling that I was on hold. Again.

Every call seemed like a round of medical roulette. Would I get the sympathetic assistant who'd been on the job for a decade and knew the system inside out? Or the newbie, stumbling over which button to press, only to accidentally hang up, plunging me back into the tedious cycle of redialing and explaining my situation from scratch?

In between the to-and-fro of picking up files and requesting appointments, I thought about how I would narrate this story. While I've always been candid about my life in my social media posts, something made me hold back on sharing my diagnosis. Hesitation had settled in, not because of fear, but due to the sheer magnitude of the story unfolding. I sensed there were more layers to this narrative than I had uncovered so far, and it still wasn't time to invite others in.

Yet, beneath the tumult of emotions (and the whirlwind of medical waiting rooms), there surged a potent undercurrent of determination. It was a force so compelling that I decided to put words to it.

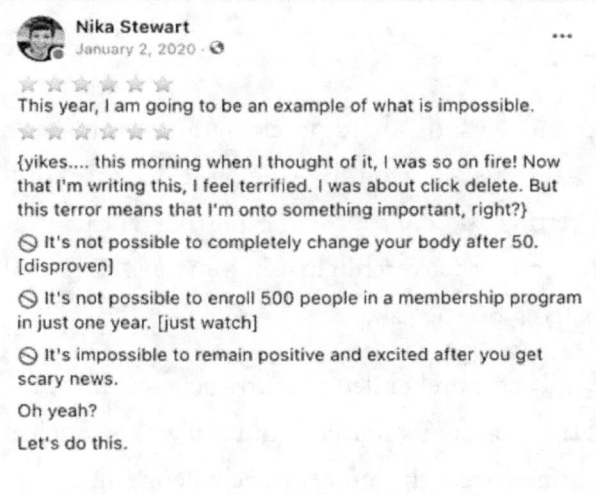

This year, I am going to be an example of what is impossible.

{yikes…. this morning when I thought of it, I was so on fire! Now that I'm writing this, I feel terrified. I was about click delete. But this terror means that I'm onto something important, right?}

🚫 *It's not possible to completely change your body after 50.*

[disproven]

🚫 *It's not possible to enroll 500 people in a membership program in just one year. [just watch]*

🚫 *It's impossible to remain positive and excited after you get scary news.*

Oh yeah?
Let's do this.

Going public with this bold proclamation was more than just catharsis—it was a beacon. By voicing it, I was solidifying my resolve, setting the course for the journey ahead. And if my audacity served as a torchlight for someone else's path, well, that was icing on the cake.

I hadn't fully comprehended the intricacies of the battle ahead, nor had the treatments started, but I knew this much: I had to find the inner strength to meet the challenge ahead.

I began to understand that exemplifying the impossible isn't conceivable without adversity.

During times of tranquility, when the stars align in our favor, we aren't being tested. Such periods, though comforting, lack the force that truly empowers our spirit.

To wear the badge of doing the "impossible," I realized I needed to not just face, but *relish* adversity.

Relishing hard times? I know it sounds counterintuitive.

It's not easy to get excited about tough situations. So, sometimes I deliberately dwell on past adversities. I replay the fatigue, the hurdles, the overwhelming emotions, and then bask in the transformative growth that blossomed from those tribulations. It's a reminder—a testament—that challenges are but catalysts in our journey of evolution.

Thank goodness for adversities!

Discover the unexpected treasures in your journey.
Access our exclusive Hidden Gems app, designed to help you
uncover and cherish the power in your adversity.
www.actuallyicanbook.com

ADVERSITY DODGE BALL

Life can feel like an endless game of dodgeball. Sometimes we're smacking down challenges, and sometimes it feels as if every ball is aiming straight for us.

But what if, instead of constantly ducking or swerving, we catch the ball and own it?

Recently, as I was exploring virtual workshops, a certain title grabbed my attention.

"Make Imposter Syndrome Your Friend."

"Imposter Syndrome" is a term that's probably tattooed somewhere in the psyche of every woman. That nagging voice whispering, *You're a phony. Today's the day they'll all find out. Every achievement you ever had was a fluke and every accolade you received was sheer luck.*

As someone who makes a living empowering other women to empower themselves, I've crossed paths with countless strategies to tackle this issue.

But befriending it? This was new territory. I eagerly joined the class.

The insights I received were exactly what the doctor ordered. Well, not *my* doctor. He was too busy to order any insights.

When it was my turn to get one-on-one coaching, the trainer

asked me a question. "When your Imposter Syndrome speaks to you, what does she say?"

I confessed that when I am speaking or coaching—even on topics where I have a lot of experience and success, I often worry that there are experts out there who know more than me and have more experience, so I feel that I'm not really qualified.

I expected the typical pep talk of "But you *are* qualified, you *are* good enough."

Instead, he hit me with some profound honesty.

"That voice is telling the truth."

This was unexpected. Every book I had read and training I had done recommended gaining more confidence to conquer the false voice of Imposter Syndrome.

He continued. "There *are* experts who know more than you, who have more experience than you." Think of it like breakfast, he said. In the past week, which of your breakfasts has been the best in the world?

Not every meal needs to be a gourmet extravaganza to be satisfying. Similarly, not being the top expert in your field doesn't invalidate your expertise or worth. Every expert brings a different background with unique insights to the table. While some may have more experience than you, you have just as much value to offer the world in your own unique style.

Boom. It was a lightbulb moment. Instead of fighting the Imposter Syndrome voice, I would thank her for being in my life, attempting to protect me from penetrating the borders of my comfort zone. I could listen to her, accept what she was saying, and move forward *with* her.

And just like making Imposter Syndrome my friend, I was learning to navigate the intricacies of my health journey without pushing against the tide.

If I see these complications as companions on my journey, rather than adversaries, I empower myself to rise above and truly shine.

Aikido is a Japanese martial art that emphasizes the use of an opponent's energy and movements to overcome them, rather than directly opposing them with brute force. This mindset can also apply to adversity in everyday life. Instead of fighting against a difficult situation, we can work with its energy. By doing so, we are able to not only transform a challenge into an opportunity for growth and learning, but actually enjoy the adventure.

After what felt like years packed into days, a ray of hope emerged—a message from my gynecologist, recommending a particular breast surgeon.

But would she have an available appointment soon? And was she on my insurance's approved list?

The fact that I was selecting a specialist for something as crucial as cancer based on such a restrictive list still enrages me. While I had reasonably good health insurance, being a self-employed entrepreneur meant I had to secure it on my own. There wasn't an employer-subsidized plan given to me, nor the benefits of a vast group policy. So if I didn't want to lose my house and savings, I had to choose a doctor in my network.

When I found out Dr. Camal was not only in my network, but could see me in two days, I realized that my gynecologist had handed me a treasure map, with a giant X marking the answer to my prayers.

TEENY TINY CANCER DOT

Rob drove me and my tiny, inconsequential, easy-to-remove-like-a-haircut cancer dot to Dr. Camal's office.

On entering the empty waiting room, I noticed the onslaught of pink ribbons on the walls, and an unexpected realization dawned on me. "Oh. I've officially joined this ribbon club. That's so weird."

As we waited, I tried to push away the sudden feeling of out-of-place-ness. Here I was, with what I understood was a minor glitch on the cancer spectrum, and yet I was surrounded by symbols that seemed to speak of much larger battles. I felt a blush of embarrassment for wasting the doctor's valuable time with my minor nuisance dot, when she could be focusing her talents on the women who really needed it.

On the other hand, *I* needed support. And I was still confused.

But the moment we walked into the doctor's inner office, I felt at ease.

Dr. Camal's extremely soothing and welcoming demeanor gave me immediate confidence in her experience and expertise.

She agreed that a miniscule malignancy could be addressed with a lumpectomy. And because Mother Nature had decided to place my tiny troublemaker in an accessible spot, reconstruction would likely be unnecessary. With her assurances, I mentally prepared for a straight-forward, no-fuss procedure.

A haircut.

But . . .

Dr. Camal had more to say.

According to the assessment sent over by the biopsy center, my lymph nodes were singing a cancer-free tune—a sign that the renegade cells hadn't moved on to other parts of my body. Great news, right?

Well, not exactly.

She pointed out a teeny tiny asterisk, a casual aside on the test results, sort of like an "oh, by the way" afterthought.

It turns out that while the report innocuously declared that no cancer was present in the node, it also casually mentioned that no actual node sample was taken.

No node sample was taken.

Wait, what?

To paint a clearer picture, biopsy legend Donna had sampled the area *near* the nodes, but not the node itself. That's like drilling for oil next to the well, being surprised when you don't hit a gusher, and then confidently stating there is no oil in the well.

Hall-of-Famer Donna had performed an entire concerto in

the wrong arena!

I'd say that's quite an impressive oversight.

Next came a revelation that was more of a plot twist than an actual medical update.

(Cue dramatic music)

That teensy-weensy dot, one tenth of a millimeter, was merely the size of the sample taken. *Not* the actual expanse of the cancer.

You see, when Donna had inquired about the size of my cancer, I could only relay the details from her sample report. A medical technician would (should) know that.

So, why did she indicate that was the extent of the cancer? Taking her words to heart, I believed my cancer was but a minor blip.

Looking back on Donna's glowing reputation, it seemed somewhat ironic. I mean, was missing the mark the epitome of biopsy expertise? How else could the disparity between her acclaim and my experience make sense?

Then, like a jigsaw piece finally clicking into place, Donna's earlier insistence on taking aggressive measures for my seemingly harmless tiny dot began to gel.

I believe it wasn't just overenthusiasm or concern for my well-being. Behind those confident gestures and words, I think Donna was, in her own unique way, trying to sound the alarm. She knew she had made a mistake, but hoped to guide me in the right direction without admitting her blunder.

But speculations aside, now I had a bigger concern. What did this mean for my cancer dot and the next steps in my journey?

Given the glaring omissions in my biopsy report, we were still attempting to piece together the full narrative. I felt like we hadn't moved forward in any way. After weeks of testing, we were still at a maddening standstill and now having to start all over at square one.

How extensive was this invader? Was it on the march or just holding its ground? Was this a race against time, or more of a watchful waiting game?

Dr. Camal said we need more biopsies. Given the lackluster effort at the initial testing center, she prescribed a different facility.

I felt frustrated to be starting over.

I felt annoyed at the incompetence and neglect.

And I felt amused that I was having a setback during a setback. That's a little comical, isn't it?

So as I felt the anguish and hopelessness course through my veins, I took a step back to reevaluate my narrative. I could have easily allowed my mind to trail off into a dark corner and let the misery of my circumstance consume me.

Instead, I was struck by the intense irony of Donna's reputation in contrast to reality, and I couldn't help but laugh.

Rob was apparently on the same wavelength, as he looked at me and whispered, "Thank God we had Donna doing the biopsy. A less competent technician would have biopsied your ankle."

We shared a hearty chuckle, completely out of place in such a serious situation, but exactly what was needed!

Top 10 powerful thoughts to choose during an unexpected setback:

1. What is funny about this?
2. I wonder what awesome lesson this will teach me.
3. What is the silver lining of this challenge?
4. I'm excited to learn things that I can teach others.
5. Each time I overcome an obstacle, I become more powerful.
6. I get to choose how I feel about this.
7. Thank you, Life, for keeping me on my toes.
8. I look forward to growing through this.
9. What a great opportunity to prove *actually, I can* do this.
10. Since I must go through this, why not have fun?
11. Bonus: How can I share this experience with my friends and followers?

Want more tools to help navigate life's challenges? Visit our resource page for a treasure trove of tools, exercises, and meditations, all crafted to complement your journey through Actually I Can. www.actuallyicanbook.com

A REAL BIOPSY

Stepping into this new center, I immediately sensed the shift. Or maybe I'd convinced myself this place was different because it had to be. It just had to be.

Whether or not the air was truly humming with competence and compassion, or it was just my decision to perceive that, optimism filled me.

The attentiveness of the staff took me aback. From the receptionist, who greeted me by name before I even introduced myself, to the nurse who laughed with me at the incorrect sizing of the robes, the place resonated with a sense of personal touch.

In the procedure room, the head technician, Cindy, explained the procedure. She spoke with clarity and compassion, ensuring I was comfortable and informed every step of the way.

And there were lots of steps along the way, because she took several samples of each spot that Dr. Camal was concerned about.

As the series of tests proceeded, it felt like a team working seamlessly, each member playing their role with utmost precision. There was a stark difference in their thoroughness. Each sample, each image, each moment came with a clear intent— to get the complete story.

After an intense hour, filled with sixteen encore biopsies, Cindy chatted with me about possibilities. She talked to me about what I might learn and the options I had available. She asked me questions and listened when I had questions.

Because Dr. Camal had requested biopsies of several other areas of my breast, Cindy asked about my thoughts and what I would prefer to do if, in fact, more cancer was found in these other areas.

Would I choose to do several lumpectomies to save my breast, rather than a full mastectomy?

I needed more information.

What I learned was that when breast cancer is surgically removed during a lumpectomy, a rim of normal tissue surrounding the tumor is also removed. This rim is called a margin.

Margins help show whether or not the whole tumor was removed.

The tissue removed during surgery is studied to determine if the margins contain cancer cells. If they do, more surgeries may be needed.

Because we were testing several areas of my breast, there was a potential that I'd need more than one lumpectomy.

I told Cindy that I wouldn't opt to save my breast if it meant several surgeries and many holes and extensive reconstruction.

This is the first time I had accepted that I might have to re-move my whole breast.

I had the opportunity to digest that thought as I waited for the new biopsy results.

HARNESSING MY POWER

These new results painted a completely different picture, a picture showing too vast a territory of my breast under siege to save it with a simple procedure.

There was cancer present in several areas. And yes, in fact, in addition to my infiltrated breast, the two sampled lymph nodes revealed cancer was present, as well.

My small dot, originally cast in a secondary role, had rather dramatically escalated her stage presence. What had started as a whisper of a possibility for a minor lumpectomy had crescendoed into a roaring chorus. A simple haircut was no longer an option. These new results indicated that a total mastectomy was in order.

My right breast's role in this chapter of my life was now on the brink of an unexpected curtain call.

Amidst the blur of information and the prognosis that the cancer was not only in my breast, I was ushered into another level of this grim reality as Dr. Camal referred me to an oncologist.

An oncologist.

The word sent chills down my spine. Oncologists were meant for other people, not for me.

And yet, intertwined with the chilling dread, I felt that peculiar sensation I'd experienced the moment I laid eyes on those cancer pamphlets—the flutter of a page turning to a new chapter.

I recognized the onset of a new emotion on my journey taking hold—excitement.

It was wild, inconceivable even. Excitement? At a moment like this?

Again, I know. Only a madwoman would feel excited about such a prognosis.

But in that seeming madness lay a counterintuitive wisdom. Often, it's in the face of our most formidable adversities that we find our wildest creativity, our deepest strengths, our most innovative ideas.

When pushed to the brink, when every traditional instinct screams at you to follow the common stages of despair, taking an unconventional stance can be liberating.

By embracing the journey with a mix of trepidation and excitement, I wasn't ignoring the gravity of my situation; I was harnessing its power.

Instead of letting fear consume me, I chose to dance with it, to find strength in the unpredictable whirlwind of emotions. It was my counterintuitive weapon against the most counterintuitive of circumstances.

But despite my excitement about the journey ahead, I realized the news I was receiving was incomplete. If the cancer had spread to my lymph nodes, could it have traveled further? Were my organs in danger? Had the cancer grown to where it was untreatable?

My mind reeled as I thought about the possibilities. This had grown from a minor nuisance to a serious, potentially life-threatening condition, and the most disconcerting part was that we still did not know the extent of the diagnosis. Without that knowledge, there was no way to create a game plan.

This was the period of time when Rob and I were most uncertain and fearful about my future.

Enter Dr. Horkheimer

Rob and I walked into the cancer center, and I was still feeling out of my element. Was this my new identity? Or might this still be a quick event that I would soon look back on? Like that haircut.

I furtively looked around the waiting room, trying not to intrude on anyone's private space, but I wondered what each person was doing here. It couldn't be for good reasons.

And I realized they might be wondering about me.

Did they think I belonged here? Did I?

Dr. Horkheimer greeted us in a small room, and I immediately felt grateful to have him as my new guide on this bewildering journey. His calm and confident demeanor was like a gentle wind that extinguished each fireball of fear we threw at him.

Of all our concerns, Rob finally asked the biggest question of all: Are you confident that you can treat this cancer?

We received a response that will forever be etched on my heart. "No, that's not the plan at all," Dr. Horkeimer stated matter-of-factly.

Our hearts sank. What does he mean that isn't the plan? Is my cancer untreatable?

"We're not going to treat this cancer. We're going to *cure* it."

But while he was able to allay our immediate fears, he couldn't yet illuminate the entire path ahead.

Would there be multiple operations? Would I need to brace for a scary trek through chemotherapy? Would radiation be my route?

The treatment map remained fuzzy, as we still needed more information.

Before we could even think about plotting the next part of the journey, we had to extract the intruder. Every cell needed to be analyzed. The impending mastectomy was not just a medical procedure, but an information-gathering mission, setting the stage for what would follow.

So I scheduled a mastectomy for a few weeks later. The breast that had been one half of the "Best Breasts in the Dorm" would no longer be.

THE BIG REVEAL

Suddenly, I knew it was time to share my adventure.

At this point, I had only confided in a few close friends and family members. And now I now had everything I needed to reveal the full story to other friends, colleagues, clients, and acquaintances. And I also felt I could infuse my journey with optimism, joy, and humor—my personal brand—and invite my online community along.

In the business world, there's a ubiquitous piece of advice: "Don't share the wound." It's a protective notion suggesting that people should wait until their tribulations are over, thus presenting their tales as finished masterpieces of resilience. The belief is that sharing the raw, unfiltered moments of adversity can project weakness.

But I wondered, isn't it *vulnerability* that makes us undeniably human? Doesn't authenticity connect us and allow us to truly trust each other?

Wouldn't genuineness make a person *more* attractive and trustworthy?

While scrolling through my online feeds, I'd often come across neatly packaged narratives—success stories dotted with obstacles that had long been overcome, life lessons handily tied up with a ribbon of wisdom. As inspiring as many of these stories were, they sometimes felt distant, unrelatable, and almost always unattainable.

They lacked the chaotic beauty of the present moment, the raw, *real* emotions of living through a challenge.

I wanted to flip the script.

In the online world, we tend to curate the best versions of ourselves. But I had come to realize that true strength lies in letting the mask fall away. If we allow our community to witness our journey, the hardships and triumphs, the moments of courage and doubt, the bonds that form are indescribably powerful.

My decision to publicly and boldly reveal my hardship felt right, even if business gurus recommended otherwise.

The past hours, days, and weeks of contemplation about how and when I would share my situation culminated in a single resolve. My story deserved to be heard in real-time, not just as a retrospective.

My digital odyssey commenced when I hit "post" on this Facebook status update, revealing my diagnosis and imminent mastectomy.

> *I feel like it's time to share what I've been going through for the past 4 weeks. I'll start with the good news...*
>
> *I'm having a mastectomy.*
>
> *(Yes! You can imagine how scary things seemed for that to be good news 😣)*

I'll also say that I am feeling not only physically great, but emotionally fine. Actually - strangely - I feel wonderful. (This may change in the next few days as we get closer to surgery, but for now...)

The hardest thing I've gone through in the past month is *waiting* (setting appointments, more tests, waiting for results, more tests) - with no answers and no clear path or schedule.

But now I seem to have a tentative schedule for surgery next week. So this week I'll be diving in deep to do as much work as I can. Luckily I have an amazing work team to care for our clients, and an amazing life team to take care of me 😣

That singular act of vulnerability turned out to be more liberating and empowering than I could have imagined.

Are you inspired to share your own story?
Head over to www.actuallyicanbook.com *for a guide on*
navigating social media with authenticity and vulnerability.
Find advice and templates to help you share your
challenges powerfully and positively.

MAKE THAT A DOUBLE

As I navigated the world of mastectomies, I learned there was another journey to embark upon—the quest for a plastic surgeon.

If I intended to have a reconstruction—and I did—there was a protocol. The plastic surgeon had to be present during the mastectomy. The breast surgeon would remove the breast and all offensive lymph nodes (which, as I later learned, is just an educated guess), and then pass the baton (or in this case, the scalpel) to the plastic surgeon to finish the procedure.

My breast surgeon, with the enthusiasm of a friend recommending a favorite hairdresser, suggested a plastic surgeon she had frequently teamed up with for these occasions.

The catch?

My insurance didn't include her in their network. Paying for this procedure was not an option, as the cost could easily reach multiple six figures.

And just like that, I was back in the maddening marathon of making calls, rallying for last-minute consultations, and pleading with my insurance company, hoping they'd bend their rigid rules just this once.

In a miraculous twist of events, all the pieces of this intricate puzzle began to align.

My insurance company, for once, displayed a burst of empathy and gave the green light to the very plastic surgeon I had been angling for.

Not to be outdone in generosity, Dr. Griffith, the busy surgeon, reshuffled her bustling calendar to be present for my mastectomy—which was now just one week away.

The gears of the healthcare machine, notorious for their grinding slowness, suddenly sped up and began slotting into place.

So there I was, just days away from the procedure, in Dr. Griffith's office, laden with all sorts of brochures and samples (my journey was littered with pamphlets!). My mind was abuzz with choices.

First, we discussed implants. What type? What shape? What size? Then there was the option of the natural route—using my own body tissue to reform a breast. It felt like being in an ice cream shop with too many flavors. I love having choices, but whenever there is an important decision to make, I tend to get overwhelmed and afraid that I will make a mistake. This was a selection I had to get right the first time.

Delaying the procedure wasn't an option I was keen on. Every tick-tock of the clock was a sharp reminder of the not-so-tiny-anymore dot residing within me. Yet, the weight of the impending decision about reconstruction felt paralyzing.

Dr. Griffith took away that stress.

She told me I needn't make a concrete decision on the exact nature of reconstruction right then. I learned that during the mastectomy, she would install an expander, a placeholder where my new breast would eventually reside. Over the subsequent months, this expander would gradually be filled with a liquid until it mirrored the size of my other breast. Then I would have a procedure to replace the expander.

Ultimately, whether I wanted an implant or to go the organic route using my tissue and fat would be a decision I could make in the coming months.

A palpable relief washed over me.

However, just as I thought my decision-making was complete, another crossroad presented itself.

As I continued to chat with the doctor, an unexpected narrative unfolded. Her PA, Mary, revealed that she, too, had danced with cancer. Only one breast was positive, but when confronted with the thought of unevenness in her breasts post-reconstruction, she'd chosen a path some would call drastic. She made the decision to have both breasts removed!

My initial reaction?

Absolute disbelief.

It seemed like an extreme measure just to ensure symmetry.

Dr. Griffith was straightforward. Achieving perfect symmetry between a natural and a reconstructed breast was a tall order.

With clothes on? Fairly indistinguishable. But naked? There'd be visual disparities.

Internally, I battled.

Could I . . . *would I* really consider removing a perfectly healthy breast just for symmetry's sake? The very thought felt like vanity knocking on the doors of madness. And yet, I heard an unspoken whisper of consideration.

However, the next revelation was the twist I hadn't anticipated. Upon removing both her breasts, Mary's "healthy" one had revealed cancerous cells lurking beneath the surface.

This revelation felt eerily familiar, as I realized I'd heard this story elsewhere.

I needed to know. "Is this common?"

The nod I received was gravely affirmative.

I learned that women who have cancer in one breast often have minuscule amounts of cancer in the other, so tiny they go unnoticed. These are treacherous invisible seeds that are primed to blossom into something more menacing with time if left unchecked.

With a daunting journey that included a mastectomy and other treatments ahead of me, it was hard to imagine doing this all over again a few months or years down the line!

Suddenly, the notion of removing both breasts wasn't about

vanity. It was about being preemptive. Removing both breasts was not only cautionary, it now seemed like the smart move to make.

Should I have both breasts removed?

With the sands of time slipping rapidly through my fingers, I needed to quickly make this heavy decision. I had a few days to let the breast surgeon know of my choice.

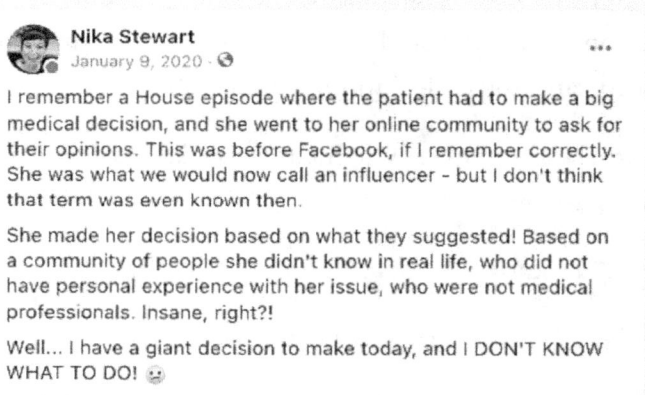

Nika Stewart
January 9, 2020 · 🌐

I remember a House episode where the patient had to make a big medical decision, and she went to her online community to ask for their opinions. This was before Facebook, if I remember correctly. She was what we would now call an influencer - but I don't think that term was even known then.

She made her decision based on what they suggested! Based on a community of people she didn't know in real life, who did not have personal experience with her issue, who were not medical professionals. Insane, right?!

Well... I have a giant decision to make today, and I DON'T KNOW WHAT TO DO! 😕

⭕😾👍 21   43 Comments

I remember a House episode where the patient had to make a big medical decision, and she went to her online community to ask for their opinions. This was before Facebook, if I remember correctly. She was what we would now call an influencer - but I don't think that term was even known then.

She made her decision based on what they suggested! Based

on a community of people she didn't know in real life, who did not have personal experience with her issue, who were not medical professionals. Insane, right?!

Well... I have a giant decision to make today, and I DON'T KNOW WHAT TO DO! 😕

I seriously did not know what to do.

Well, okay—here is the truth.

My whole being was telling me to choose to have a double mastectomy. But I was fighting it because I thought I might be making that choice for vain reasons.

I did not want to be someone who removes a breast just so I could look better after the reconstructive plastic surgery.

I thought I was looking for justifications to remove my breast. That I was pretending I should remove my "healthy" breast because I thought it might not be healthy, even though I was really just being extremely shallow.

I wanted to choose to have a double mastectomy. But I didn't want to choose it for the wrong reasons.

I didn't trust myself, and I wasn't giving myself permission to make the decision I wanted to make.

And no one wanted to give me their opinions. After all, it was a major, life-altering decision (not like a haircut).

My husband said he supported me in whatever decision I made.

My mother said she supported me in whatever decision I made.

My friends said they supported me in whatever decision I made.

That's very nice. But I wanted someone to TELL ME WHAT DECISION TO MAKE.

So I did what I know how to do—I went on social media to crowdsource the answer.

I had joined a breast cancer support group, and I posted about my dilemma and asked for opinions and experience.

Nika Stewart
January 9, 2020 ·

Hello friends. I am having a mastectomy on Monday (lobular carcinoma), and I need to decide if it should be a double. The left breast looks clean, and I have no family history. There isn't enough time to get gene test results. I'm 51 years old.

Doctor says either decision is the right decision. I keep going back and forth! How do I make this decision?

Renee Hanania and 11 others   198 Comments

Hello friends. I am having a mastectomy on Monday (lobular carcinoma), and I need to decide if it should be a double. The left breast looks clean, and I have no family history. There isn't enough time to get gene test results. I'm 51 years old.

Doctor says either decision is the right decision. I keep going back and forth! How do I make this decision?

Obviously, I wasn't simply going to do what strangers said I should do. But I wanted to hear others' stories so I could gain clarity and make a more informed choice.

About 95% of the people who had experienced something similar said they would opt for a double mastectomy.

Why?

Either they had removed their supposedly healthy breast and found cancer, or they did *not* remove the healthy breast, and then found cancer a few years later and had to relive the entire cancer experience again.

Another important point was brought up in the group. If I decided to keep one breast, that would mean semiannual mammograms (at least), followed by near-mandatory ultrasounds, and constant self-exams checking for lumps. Did I really want to put myself through that month after month, year after year?

And what if, God forbid, cancer reared its ugly head once again a few months or years down the line? Was I really prepared to experience this trauma all over again?

After reading hundreds of stories and speaking with my breast surgeon, I made a decision.

Just three days before my surgery, I decided to remove both my breasts.

Yet, as much as I had deliberated, a lingering doubt clouded my spirit. I was anchored by a weighty concern.

My mother.

The mere thought of calling her squeezed my heart. Even—especially—in my most challenging moments, the desire for my mother's approval was strong. And because I thought she was rooting for a single mastectomy, it was going to be difficult to tell her I was opting for a double.

Taking a deep breath, I mustered the courage to dial her number. She asked if I'd made up my mind. My heart raced as I uttered the words, "I know this isn't what you wanted, but I am going to have a double mastectomy."

The pause that followed was excruciating. I waited, hoping for her blessing.

What unfolded next was unexpected.

It turns out that my mom wasn't actually leaning all the way in one direction like I thought. Instead, she was riding the same wave of ambivalence and was just as confused as everyone else.

She didn't think any decision was wrong; she was simply hoping that I made the right decision for myself.

I prepared for my surgery, feeling at peace with my decision.

FIND THE FUNNY

When I was twenty-eight years old, I was dating a man who I wanted to spend the rest of my life with. He hadn't made the same decision about me yet, but I was going to change his mind.

One evening when I arrived home to my apartment, there was a message on my answering machine* from him.

*Answering machine [an-ser-ing muh-sheen] noun (for all of you post-Gen X readers). A primitive piece of equipment that recorded telephone messages for when you couldn't answer the phone. It used "cassette tapes" that you would rewind to play back your messages. Reaching the height of popularity in the 80s, this antiquated technology became obsolete when the Macarena went mainstream.

"Nika, I'm not feeling great. If you call me and I'm not here, I'm in the hospital."

Gulp.

He didn't have a cell phone (this was before the world owned mobile phones), so I called his place and he didn't answer. I then called the local hospital and asked if he was there. I was put on hold for what felt like a half hour.

"Yes, he's here," a woman came on the phone and said.

"Should I come there to see him? Or will he be home soon?"

"Oh, no," she said. "He's going to be here a while."

Double gulp.

I ran to my car and began driving to the emergency room. When I realized I wasn't sure how to get there, I suddenly remembered an incident from a few years earlier.

I'd been driving to a show. I was part of a cast of actors performing at a club. We were all meeting at the producer's house an hour before the event so we could rehearse one more time, then drive to the performance.

But as I slowed down to stop for a red light, my car died. It simply shut off. I was stuck at the light. And it was getting dark.

Before cell phones, this occurrence meant we had to rely on the kindness of strangers. Thank goodness, a woman behind me pulled up next to me to see if I needed help. She said she would drive to the next gas station and call the police. How lovely! But would she really do that? It meant going out of her way and taking extra time.

There are many days when I wonder how any of us survived without mobile phones. If this happened today, and I didn't have my phone with me, I would be beside myself with panic. But what could I do? I simply sat and waited.

Miraculously, within a half hour, a police car showed up, *followed by my parents!* Apparently, the angel who had called the police told them my license plate number. They looked it up, saw my dad listed as the owner of the car, and called him.

Not only did my dad drive to me, but my mom came behind him in *her* car. They knew I had to be somewhere, and so they brought me a car to use while *they* waited for the tow truck.

Okay, besides the fact that I have the most thoughtful, amazing parents in the world, this whole incident led to my father encouraging me to get a "car phone." His little girl was going out a lot at night. I was performing in a band and with a theatrical company, plus I was in my twenties and single, so I had both the energy and the desire to stay out late. My dad was worried. A phone in my car would put his mind at ease.

My parents got me my very own car phone, a clunky, cumbersome apparatus whose receiver was bigger than my head! It was, nonetheless, an important piece of equipment that put my and my parents' minds at ease.

So here I was, in the pre-everyone-in-the-world-owns-a-smartphone era, driving to the hospital to check on my boyfriend, and not knowing how to get there. But I had a phone, so I called a friend.

While I bit my nails and tried to stop my legs from shaking, he gave me directions.

I parked and ran into the hospital, desperately searching for my love. I saw him lying on a bed, thrashing around in pain.

What the heck was going on?

A doctor was talking to him. I hid behind a curtain and heard the doctor tell him he was having a heart attack.

Huh? A heart attack? He was thirty-three years old. He was too young to have a heart attack. I was twenty-eight. I was too young to have a boyfriend who was having a heart attack.

But yes. This was apparently a massive heart attack. And they needed to give him life-saving medicine to control it right away.

As the medicine started to work, they moved him to an area where I could stand next to him. The pain eased, and he stopped thrashing. When the doctor came over to explain the situation, my boyfriend pointed to me and said, "If you need to use the paddles, I want *her* to be the one to yell, CLEAR!"

We all smiled. His sense of humor eased the tension.

The next few weeks were scary. But I can't imagine how much worse it would have been if we hadn't all found ways to laugh.

Spoiler alert: twenty-five years later, this man—now my husband—is still making me laugh. How lucky am I?

Healing with Humor

In the rollercoaster of life, I've often sought solace in humor. And while I've personally felt the benefits, there's science—solid, empirical research—to back up the notion that humor is not only psychologically uplifting but also genuinely thera-peutic on a physiological level.

Laughter has been scientifically proven to:

- **Reduce Blood Pressure** – Say goodbye to those antihy-pertensive meds! Okay, not really, but you get the drift.
- **Decrease Heart and Respiratory Rate** – Taking care of the ticker and those lungs.
- **Relieve Pain:** Studies have shown laughter can be as effective as some painkillers!
- **Boost the Immune System** – Laughter cuts down on those pesky stress hormones while amplifying immune cells and those fantastic infection-fighting antibodies.
- **Uplift the Mind** – Besides reducing anxiety and de-pression, laughter triggers the release of endorphins, our body's built-in happy pills.
- **Promote Cardiac Health** – It doesn't just protect the heart by reducing stress. Laughter actively improves blood vessel function and promotes healthy blood flow.

But the benefits of laughter go even deeper. Research has shown that a genuine guffaw mellows the entire body, keeping muscles relaxed for up to forty-five minutes post-laughter.

If you're having a conflict, find humor in the situation. Laugh-ter lightens the dense weight of anger and frustration, allow-ing confrontations to fizzle out without lingering bitterness or grudges.

Then, there's longevity. A study from Norway discovered that individuals with a robust sense of humor generally outlived those who didn't laugh as often. This difference became particularly striking among those battling illnesses such as cancer!

Humor can diminish pain and give us relief from stress and worry. Studies have shown that laughter significantly reduces anxiety, depression, and overall stress.

And a sense of humor even lowers mortality rates!

So, when Rob and I laughed at the insanity of my biopsy results, we weren't making light of the situation. It was therapy, it was medicine, and above all, it was a celebration of life.

Embracing laughter has been one of my secret weapons, not just to get through the tough times, but to thrive.

But wait. How do you find the funny in cancer?

Well, for me, I embraced the absurdity of my situation and laughed at myself. A few days before my double mastectomy, I posted this:

51-year-old bra model available.
(Limited time only 😕)

I discovered that when I laughed, when I shared the humorous aspects of what I was going through, when I acted silly and funny, I gave everyone around me permission to laugh. And when everyone is laughing with me, there's little room for negative energy.

As my treatments went on and side effects grew stronger, it was a blessing to have all the positive energy surrounding me.

*Laughter is a powerful tool (and it's just so fun!).
If you're looking to lighten your load with humor, you can
access exclusive comedic journal prompts on our site.
The 'Find the Funny' journal is designed to bring a smile to
your face, even on the toughest days.*
www.actuallyicanbook.com

It's important to note that finding humor in difficult situations doesn't mean we are downplaying the severity of our struggles. It's still essential to address and work through them in a healthy way. But by finding the humor in our challenges, we can create a sense of levity and make them feel less overwhelming.

Take a moment to think about some of the greatest challenges in your life. Could you take a step back to find the funny? Is there a way you can lighten your load by injecting laughter into the situation?

Often, we've heard comedians offer jokes following tragic events around the world. When met with just a few titters in the audience, we sometimes hear the comedian say, "Too soon?" Well, I am here to say, "It's not too soon!" Finding the funny in trying times does not mean you are dismissing the gravity of the situation; rather, you are using laughter as a coping mechanism to preserve your mental health and find healthy ways to deal with adversity.

MASTECTOMY

Have you ever played that game of "What If," speculating how you might react if life threw you the curveball you've heard about but never personally experienced?

Whenever I heard about someone learning they had cancer, there was a description of going numb, not being able to listen, and lots of tears.

I always assumed I'd be composed if I ever heard that terrifying news.

Throughout most of the early stages of my journey, I felt as if I was still in this hypothetical stage, as if it were not yet real.

On the day before my surgery, my home was filled with preparations and decisions.

I'm always so chilly. Will the hospital bed be warm enough or do I need to bring my own blanket?

I'm packing my toiletries for the overnight stay, but will I be able to get up to take care of myself?

My small suitcase sat by my bedroom door, hinting at the looming event, but inside, I felt an unexpected calm.

During my packing, my cousin Robin called. Over the phone, she asked, "How are you holding up?" Her voice was tinged with concern.

"I'm doing really well," I replied quickly. Then I recognized how crazy that sounded. But I was sincere.

As I hung up, I pondered my sense of peace.

Then I realized I was still thinking hypothetically.

In other words, I was still acting as if I didn't know what was going to happen.

I wasn't feeling scared or sad (or worse) about the upcoming surgery to remove my breasts because I still believed it was only a *possibility*.

I was still in a place of, *I wonder what it would be like for me if I had to go through this?*

I stared at myself in the mirror. An important part of my body was going to be removed. I didn't need breasts to function, but they were a huge part of my identity!

I was always the girl with the big boobs. I mean, I had won "Best Breasts in the Dorm!" (Oh, did I mention that before? 😕)

Was I in denial? Or was I really okay?

As I attempted to gather my feelings, I shared an update with my Facebook friends.

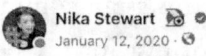

Nika Stewart 🐾 ✓
January 12, 2020 · 🌐

In college I won "Best Breasts in the Dorm" 🏛 which was totally sexist, very silly, and... extremely flattering.

I've always been on the large side, and my breasts have been a big part of my identity (I assume that's true for most women). But - although I admit I'm as vain as (probably vainer than) anyone else, I really think I'm going to be okay after they are removed tomorrow.

In the last few days, I realize that I've been thinking "hypothetically." Like - how would I feel if this was happening to me? Well, hypothetically I think I would be okay.

But realistically? 😔 I really think I'm going to be okay.

In college I won "Best Breasts in the Dorm" 😔 *which was totally sexist, very silly, and... extremely flattering.*

I've always been on the large side, and my breasts have been a big part of my identity (I assume that's true for most women). But - although I admit I'm as vain as (probably vainer than) anyone else, I really think I'm going to be okay after they are removed tomorrow.

In the last few days, I realize that I've been thinking "hypothetically." Like - how would I feel if this was happening to me? Well, hypothetically I think I would be okay.

But realistically? 😔 *I really think I'm going to be okay.*

Indeed, I felt okay.

Why? How did this sense of okayness surround me, especially at such a tumultuous moment?

I wasn't entirely sure. Yet.

Luckily, I was granted an extended voyage ahead, one that

would inevitably unravel the intricacies of this strange mind-set. This journey would provide insights not just for my personal comfort, but to share with those in need of unconventional strategies to face adversity head-on.

That evening, as I settled into bed, the peculiar yet now familiar sense of adventure snuggled up beside me.

Bring on tomorrow.

EMPOWERED HEALING: AN UNCONVENTIONAL CHECKLIST

Facing surgery, or any kind of trauma, either anticipated or sudden, can be daunting. The fear of the unknown, the anticipation of pain, and the potential lifestyle changes all contribute to a whirlwind of emotions.

I've been there.

In the maze of confusion and unknowns, I found something profound—an opportunity for personal growth and a chance to challenge conventional healing methods.

This checklist, rooted in my journey and the philosophy of "Actually I Can," is designed to help you reframe your mindset. It isn't just a list; it's a vehicle to find not only hope, but exhilaration in adversity. Every point on this checklist has been curated with love, care, and the intention to give you control in an environment where you might feel powerless.

Every item you check off this list brings you closer to transforming a daunting trauma into an experience of joy. It's about embracing the journey, finding beauty in the process, and proving to yourself that every challenge holds a hidden gift.

Whether you're prepping for a scheduled surgery or navigating any unexpected setback, this roadmap is designed to infuse optimism into your recovery process. It's a blend of practicality, a sprinkle of unconventional wisdom, and a large dose of positivity.

I want you to see your challenge not just as a hurdle to get over, but as an event packed with potential—potential for self-discovery, growth, and inspiration. Through this list, you're not just preparing for recovery, you're focused on finding the silver linings, celebrating small wins, and inspiring others with your resilience.

I invite you to peruse this list, add to it, and modify it to best fit your needs. Take this journey one step at a time, believing in the power of your spirit.

Because, remember, "actually, you can."

Get your own editable and printable copy of the 'Empowered Healing Checklist'. Customize it, make it your own, and harness its power to enrich your healing process. Download it here: www.actuallyicanbook.com

Checklist

☐ Creative Outlets
  o Make a list of hobbies you'd love to explore
  o Take the first step in diving into your creative journey (pick up art supplies, buy a special journal, enroll in an online magic class, etc.)
  o Imagine what you will be able produce after diving into your activity for several months

☐ What skills or knowledge would you like to develop while you are recovering in bed?
  ▪ learn a new language
  ▪ research your favorite subject
  ▪ study for a new certification
  ▪ take up knitting
  o Research online courses in this subject
  o List the ways this new skills will enhance your life
  o Announce your intention to pursue this new area of study

☐ Set small goals for each day of recovery. List what you will do to savor each victory. No matter how tiny the achievement, commit to celebrating! Every win is moving forward, and every time you celebrate, you are adding joy and optimism to your life.

☐ Record a pre-surgery message. Create a video or voice note talking to your future self. Remind yourself of the strength you have and the challenges you've overcome so far.

- [ ] List the TV shows/movies to binge and their respective channels or streaming platforms to make them easy to find.
  - o Consider documentaries or an educational series that will expand your knowledge
  - o Listen to podcasts or Ted Talks that challenge the way you think
  - o Find a nostalgic TV series from your past to enjoy

- [ ] Make a list of books or e-books you've been meaning to read (stack them next to your bed/download them to easily find them).

- [ ] Make a list of tasks that can be done in bed or with minimal movement.
  - o Clear out and organize emails
  - o Write thank-you cards or messages
  - o Create an online shopping or wish list
  - o Sort digital photos
  - o Learn through online courses or tutorials (that don't require physical exertion)

- [ ] Gather not only comfortable clothes, but a few outfits that make you feel good about yourself.

- [ ] Give back.
  - o Use this time to write letters of gratitude to individuals who've impacted your life
  - o Start or plan a small fundraiser or awareness campaign related to your condition or surgery, turning your experience into a force for good

MY EXPECTED FINALE

My head was cloudy, and I struggled to focus. I sensed that my operation was over, but I didn't have the vaguest notion where I was. I tried to open my eyes but couldn't. With a dry mouth and jumbled thoughts, I managed to open my lips and say, "Am I saying this out loud, or is it just in my head?"

A couple of seconds passed before I heard a sympathetic voice respond, "Yes, honey, you're in the recovery room. I've been here with you, and I can hear you just fine."

To which I replied, "Oh good, because the last three times I asked that, no one answered."

~~

I'm not sure why I expected the mastectomy to be the culmination of my journey.

I had this image in my head: The procedure would wrap up, and I'd go home to heal, taking it easy for a few weeks, while planning for reconstruction—the prize at the end of the tunnel.

The new perky boobs I designed in my head were my silver lining. After all the trauma, I'd get to pick out a fun, youthful set that defied my age.

As with all the other jaunts on this journey, I got sideswiped.

When they finally moved me to a hospital room post-surgery, I expected to see a flat chest, and instead saw some fairly sizable bumps. Wait, were those . . . breasts? Dr. Griffith mentioned expanders, but I imagined them as placeholders that would get pumped up gradually. Guess they don't start completely flat. Well, that was news to me!

Hours passed in that hospital room.

Okay, maybe it was minutes. But it felt like forever, and I couldn't help but wonder where the heck my husband was. Although I couldn't move very well, I somehow grabbed the buzzer to call someone and ask if they could find my man.

Finally, he rushed in, looking worn out and anxious. The poor guy hadn't been told I was ready for visitors, and he was running around trying to find someone who could give him information. I was so relieved to see him. Though, if I'm honest, his frazzled appearance worried me.

He began to fill me in. Dr. Camal had hoped to find just the two cancerous nodes under my arm, but when she got in there, a lot more looked sketchy. She had to take out an entire section of nodes, only to find another bunch underneath that looked suspicious.

After removing that section, she was afraid to go further because removing too many lymph nodes could have long-term negative side effects.

She had taken out a whopping eighteen nodes! This wasn't

what we'd expected. And Rob had gotten a pessimistic feeling from the doctor.

I was in too much discomfort to fully take in the news. But poor Rob was soaking it in and he was panicked. After helping me brush my teeth (I couldn't hold a toothbrush), he left to go home to be with Ellie, our fourteen-year-old daughter.

As I tried to get comfortable and fall asleep, I thought about Ellie.

The next day, she would be competing in a mock trial as the lead attorney at the county courthouse, an event she had prepared and rehearsed for months. Here was an experience I wouldn't be able to witness, a memory I wouldn't share with her. Maternal guilt took over. Yet, even in my vulnerability, gratitude became my stronghold.

My heart swelled with appreciation, knowing that even if I couldn't be there, she wasn't alone. Rob, always Ellie's hero, would be by her side. And my dad, her Papa, with his endless wisdom and infectious enthusiasm, would cheer her on from the side. Imagining them there, supporting her, eased the sting of my absence.

But more than that, the very thought of Ellie, with her unwavering strength and independence, comforted me. My sweet baby wasn't so little anymore.

I wanted to model strength and resilience for my daughter. But I knew she already had that inside her.

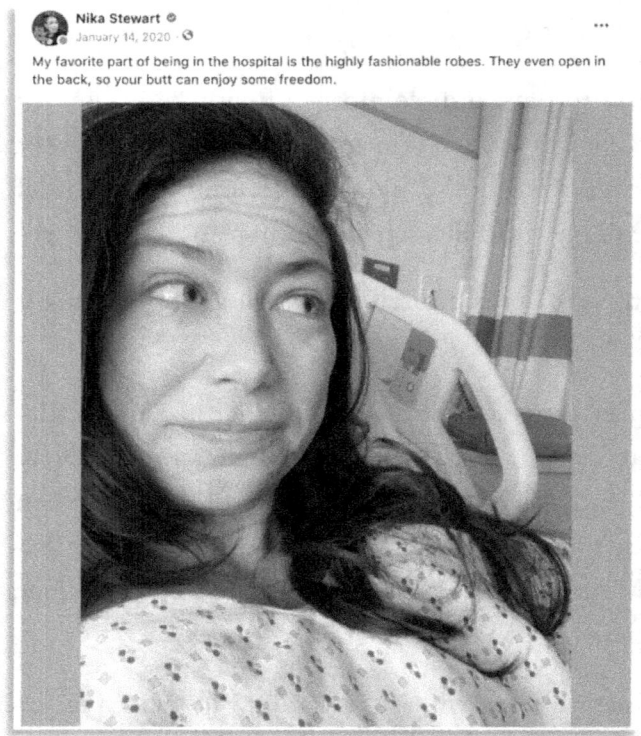

My favorite part of being in the hospital is the highly fashionable robes. They even open up in the back, so your butt can enjoy some freedom.

LET'S GO HOME AND HEAL

The following days at home were, in a word, rough. Pain and Discomfort were my primary companions, and they were such needy friends that they even pushed Adventure out of the bed many times.

And the drains. Oh, the drains! They were my least favorite thing. I had three of those suckers sticking out of me, and let me tell you, there's nothing glamorous about draining and measuring body fluids throughout the day. Especially when you feel achy, tired, and in pain.

But I had my rock-star husband and my amazing daughter by my side.

In the mornings, before leaving to get on the school bus, Ellie and I stood in the corner of my bedroom so she could drain me. She squeezed each tube so lovingly, making sure not to pull in the wrong place. Then she opened the stoppers, emptied the bulbs, measured the amount of fluid, and wrote down the numbers.

And she made sure I took my morning pills, documenting each one on a spreadsheet she created.

During the day, while Ellie was in school, Rob made sure I had special treats. Muffins, coffee . . .

Now that I think of it, those don't seem like special treats. But at the time, coffee and muffins made me happy.

Oh, painkillers and kitty snuggles also helped.

Nika Stewart
January 16, 2020 · 🌐

I've discovered the answer to the universe: Pain killers and kitty cuddles. I never want to move from this position again.

221   59 Comments

I've discovered the answer to the universe: Pain killers
and kitty cuddles. I never want to move from this position
again.

Those first few days of healing became a painful blur. Well, except for the delicious meals that kept showing up on my doorstep.

BORROWING POWER

Life has a way of flipping the script on us, sometimes when we least expect it. We're used to being the giver, the doer, the strong one. Then, in a sudden twist, we find ourselves in a vulnerable spot.

I'd always considered myself fiercely independent. But after my mastectomy, I needed help with basic tasks. Imagine, for a moment, relying on someone to brush your teeth or needing assistance every time you hit the restroom. It's humbling, to say the least.

But here's the thing. When you're thrown into these moments of vulnerability, there's also a chance for profound growth and connection. We often think of ourselves as the providers of aid or the pillars of strength for others. Yet, when the tables turn, and you require help, there's a certain beauty in accepting it, despite your usual inclination to go it alone.

And that acceptance has the power to change relationships. It allows others to step up, to feel a sense of purpose, to genuinely connect. I began to see help in a new light—not as a sign of weakness, but as an opportunity for mutual empowerment. When I allowed someone to assist me, it wasn't just me benefiting from the act. The giver felt a surge of purpose and connection, too.

For instance, take the subtle raps on my door during that arduous first week post-surgery.

As I tentatively navigated my recovery, the enticing aroma of delicious meals filled my home.

Unbeknownst to me, a quartet of thoughtful local friends had orchestrated a meal train. Instead of waiting for me to reach out or express a need, they proactively designated days and indulged my family with carefully chosen, home-cooked meals, from the main course to delightful sides and delicious desserts.

Several of the meals turned out to be huge favorites, and I had to make my friends promise to give me the recipes for when I felt up to cooking.

Their spontaneous kindness illuminated an important lesson that I try to remember when others are in need.

We often extend a well-meaning, "Let me know if you need anything," assuming it's the ultimate in kindness. But in reality, when someone is weighed down by pain or struggles, such vague offers can feel overwhelming, even burdensome. The mere act of having to articulate a need can be an added stressor.

And most people will not let us know if they need anything.

My experience taught me a more compassionate approach. Instead of extending an open-ended offer, provide specific options for support.

Rather than the vague "What would you like?" or "I'm here

if you need me," try, "Can I handle school drop-offs for your kids tomorrow?"

or

"Would you prefer a homemade dinner or an order from House of Pancakes tonight?"

This nuanced shift in our approach can ease the recipient's decision-making process, turning our offer of help into meaningful comfort during their challenging times. It makes a world of difference.

Want to brighten the day of someone battling breast cancer? Visit www.actuallyicanbook.com for a thoughtful list of gifts that truly make a difference.

THE RESULTS ARE IN!

A week later, the time had arrived for our anticipated sit-down with Dr. Camal. She was ready to divulge the details of the tissues and nodes they had analyzed. A cocktail of nervousness and eagerness filled me. As much as I was concerned about the nitty-gritty of the findings, I was excitedly flipping ahead to the next chapter—reconstruction.

I had already begun daydreaming about my new set of breasts—the contour, the height, the possibilities. This was a unique opportunity to redesign, and boy, was I brimming with plans! If they thought I had "Best Breasts in the Dorm" (oh, did I mention that already? 😕), just wait'll they see me now!

I sat in the doctor's office with my arm pinned behind my back because it was the only position that eased a bit of the ache I felt on my right side. We made small talk for a minute and she told me I seemed to be putting on a brave face, but she could tell I was in pain.

For some reason, this made me think she was about to tell us everything was okay.

Instead, she hit us with a curveball. Seventeen out of the eighteen nodes she had removed were cancerous.

I immediately thought again of Donna the Legend, whose report stated that no cancer was detected in the lymph nodes. No cancer at all.

The second biopsy showed that at least two nodes were cancerous. The discovery of seventeen cancerous nodes was a shock.

What did this mean? Was the cancer now all removed?

It did not mean that.

It did mean there was a deeper story about the state of my body, and by extension, the journey I had ahead.

Dr. Camal's decision to remove only eighteen nodes was deliberate. The lymphatic system serves as our body's drainage network. It plays a crucial role in our immune response. Removing too many lymph nodes is risky, as it can lead to complications such as lymphedema, a condition where excess fluid collects in tissues, causing swelling.

This is a balancing act for surgeons. They need to remove enough nodes to determine the extent of the cancer while ensuring they don't compromise the patient's overall lymphatic function.

Dr. Camal suspected more nodes might be cancerous. By taking eighteen and finding seventeen of them affected, she deduced the gravity of the situation without having to extract more, hence minimizing potential harm. Her method was like sampling a patch of soil to determine the health of an entire field. If a significant portion of that sample is compromised, it's a strong indicator that the wider field needs attention.

This revelation meant the cancer was more widespread than initially suspected. In many ways, it was like discovering the tip of an iceberg, signaling a larger mass beneath.

Given this, the implications were clear. More aggressive and comprehensive treatments would be needed.

Dr. Camal's approach was not only thoughtful, but preservative. She ensured I got the right information with the least possible physical cost.

So yes, the number seventeen did turn my stomach into a knot. But it also made me realize how crucial it is to have a doctor who can make such discerning choices. It's about weighing the immediate against the potential, understanding the now while foreseeing the tomorrow.

"What ifs" began to play in my mind. What if we had accepted Donna's findings? What if this doctor hadn't decided to look a bit deeper? That tenacity may have saved my life.

As daunting as this discovery was, there was also immense gratitude. Now we were in the know, and armed with this knowledge, we could strategize our next steps.

Dr. Camel said my next step would likely be chemotherapy.

Chemotherapy.

The word hung in the air.

Even though I had already grappled with the diagnosis of cancer, it still felt abstract. I don't know why. After all, I had just gone through a major surgery to remove my breasts. Obviously, this was real. But the disease was happening internally, invisibly.

Chemotherapy, however? That was the real, tangible manifestation of the battle. It meant acknowledging the cancer out loud.

I know it's strange, but until this moment, I still felt like I was living an ordinary life, albeit experiencing a big, unexpected challenge.

Suddenly, it felt surreal.

It's difficult to articulate the whirlwind of sentiments that I was navigating, not because I don't have the words to describe them, but because my feelings seemed . . . out of place.

To many, what I felt will seem improbable, even impossible.

My familiar companion, Adventure, quietly entered the room, and this time, she didn't come alone. Right by her side was Excitement, flickering into the corners of my consciousness.

Crazy, right? Yes, a part of me was . . . intrigued? Eager, even? It was as if a corner of my soul whispered, "Here's another chapter. How will you write it?"

Just to assure you I'm not a robot or a relentless optimist out of touch with reality, a shadow also hung over me. A daunting shade of dread, conjured up by that one word: chemotherapy. It's an emotionally charged word laced with ominous implications, stories of pain and struggle, and, of course, the loss of hair. It was impossible to remain entirely impervious to its gravity.

So it looked like it was going to be round two with the oncologist. Strap in. The rollercoaster was far from over.

See how you can add adventure and excitement to a tough chapter in your life. Download your Story Shift workbook, filled with exercises to help you transform your perspective and your experience. www.actuallyicanbook.com

PUT DOWN THE LOAD

The atmosphere felt heavy when we exited the doctor's office. As we sat in the car, the weight of the news seeped into my body and my emotions.

Yet, as oppressive as this burden seemed, I also felt a sense of liberation tied to it.

I actually felt relief.

This load was too immense. So I had to put it down. I had the freedom to simply release it.

I had been feeling optimistic and positive, and those emotions were empowering. But they also carried a responsibility. A responsibility to be up, to be *on*. And that was getting exhausting.

Yes, I saw the silver linings. I could find lots of humor. I was truly enjoying the experience of journeying through the challenge.

At the same time, I also needed to recognize that I was human and had other emotions.

Until this moment, I had experienced two primary feelings.

Anger, which was effective for driving me into action. Action that led to getting my healthcare providers to take me seriously and open doors.

And joy, an emotion that allowed me to soar through procedures and outcomes with positivity and humor.

For the first time since the diagnosis, I chose to feel sad.

The Power of Choice

Every day we're bombarded with choices, from the most mundane decisions, like what socks to wear, to pivotal ones that might redefine our life's trajectory.

But here's the thing. Many of these choices are made subconsciously. Take your morning routine, for instance. You probably crawl out of bed the same way every day, hardly giving it a thought. It's not as if there's a supervisor instructing you to get up at the same time or eat that exact breakfast cereal. It's just what we do. Routine, predictability, the comfort of the familiar.

Yet, within these automatic choices lies a secret power—the realization that these choices are ours. We own them. Every time we subconsciously do something out of habit, we're actually making a choice.

Our thoughts? Our emotions? They're no different.

We often perceive them as random and uncontrollable. But we can, in fact, steer them. Direct them. We can opt for optimism over pessimism, or vice versa.

When my diagnosis first hit, sure, a volley of emotions bombarded me. Some were instinctive, others deliberate. Anger was my initial choice. It served as the fuel that propelled me forward, driving me to demand answers, take charge of my health, and knock down barriers.

But as the reality of surgery loomed, I pivoted. Why wallow in sorrow when I could opt for exhilaration? Why not view the surgery as an adventure? An opportunity to binge-watch that show I'd always put off? *Downton Abbey*, here I come!

With that shift in perspective, not only did I bolster my own spirits, but I also offered solace to my family, friends, and even social media followers. They no longer had to tiptoe around me, dreading potential emotional landmines.

But let's get something straight. I'm not a machine.

There were, of course, days when I felt the blues. And that's okay, too. Sometimes you need to dip into melancholy to appreciate euphoria. On those low days, I wrapped myself in the warmth of self-care, guilt free.

It's paradoxical when you think about it. When I allowed myself to fully experience sadness or lethargy, I felt better. It was like giving myself the emotional equivalent of a spa day. There's something liberating in acknowledging your feelings without the baggage of guilt.

In essence, it all boils down to this: external circumstances, those curveballs life loves to throw at us, might be out of our hands. But our internal world—the intricate dance of thoughts and emotions—that's *our* domain.

And in this arena, we have the final say. Even in the face of adversity, we can find a silver lining, a beacon of positivity, if only we choose to. It might sound bonkers, but hey, it's the kind of magic we all have within us. You just have to choose to wield it.

Get your own copy of the SHINE Emotional Mastery Playbook at www.actuallyicanbook.com

~~~

So back to sitting in the car with Rob . . .

The image of my cancer being a little speck, an insignificant dot, deteriorated. Was this more serious than I could handle?

As I started to let the sadness seep in, I blurted, "I'm going to cancel all my programs. I'll tell the members I can't continue and refund their money."

I held my breath, expecting Rob to chuckle and tell me I was overreacting. Instead, he simply said, "Okay, let's do that." There wasn't a hint of hesitation.

His agreement caught me off guard. Why wasn't he dismissing my panic?

Rob later confessed that in that vulnerable moment, he was just as worried as I was. And he wanted to support me, to show that he was with me, no matter what.

He hadn't grasped that at that particular moment the support I needed was not a "yes man," but someone to disagree with my fear. I needed a pillar of optimism.

His unexpected response was the metaphorical slap in the face I needed.

"Wait a minute," I thought to myself, "why would I shut everything down? Yes, this will probably be tough on me physically, but won't I have more great experiences to share?"

The haze of negativity started to clear. I recognized the potential in my story—the raw, real-life journey I was about to embark upon.

Chemo? That was, in a strange way, another opportunity. My experiences, my challenges, would add depth and authenticity to my work. What an incredible perspective I could offer!

This cancer journey was becoming a profound learning experience. It was an adventure I was determined to navigate and share, and in doing so, perhaps offer comfort and hope to others walking similar paths.

DANCE IN THE RAIN

It is often said that the biggest challenges in life are the ones that make us who we are. The obstacles we face can be difficult and overwhelming, but they also have the potential to teach us valuable lessons and make us stronger.

But within this lesson, we are encouraged to "tackle" the situation, "resist" the danger, "overcome" the adversity, "fight" the enemy.

What if, instead—just like I had learned to do with Imposter Syndrome—we turned the enemy into our friend?

When I was told that chemotherapy was the next necessary step to treat my spreading cancer, my first thought was, "I am going to lose my hair."

I had some choices.

I could fight it, accept it, or EMBRACE it.

Here's what *fighting* might have looked like.

I could look for ways to keep my hair—or at least, as much of it as possible. Yes, I found out, I could purchase or rent a "cold cap," a device that ices the scalp to keep the chemo drugs from affecting the hair follicles.

I would have to research this and worry about the effectiveness and the potential side effects. Worst of all, in my opinion, I'd need to sit with ice on my head for about an hour during each chemo session (which were grossly uncomfortable to begin with).

I could ask the doctor if there were variations of drugs or protocols I could implement—ones less likely to make all my hair fall out—and perhaps be less effective at killing the cancer cells.

I would have anxiety about how much hair would stay. I would worry when any fell out.

Here's what *accepting* might have looked like.

I could accept that I would lose my hair, purchase a wig that looked exactly like my everyday style, and plan to wear hats or scarves when I needed to be around people.

I could hide my baldness for eight months and wait anxiously for my hair to grow back so I could feel comfortable with myself.

This seemed like the right choice. It's what most people going through chemotherapy do.

But here's what *embracing* did look like.

As soon as I learned that I would lose my hair, I went on Pinterest to look up short hairstyles. After all, I had always wished I had the courage to try something short and sassy. Now, with my hair falling out in a month, I had nothing to lose.

I cut my hair and showed off my cute new look.

I went on Amazon and ordered a dozen wigs. I was going to have fun with my head! Green spiky hair one day, long purple waves the next.

I also enjoyed my bald head. I put on fun make-up, painted my scalp, and tried out new, unexpected looks. Why not be an edgy rock star or a funky model?

From Acceptance to Embracing

The general consensus is that we should accept the things we cannot change. Sounds logical, right? When we accept a difficult situation, we stop fighting against it and instead choose to work through it. It feels empowering to let go of resistance.

Accepting a situation means we acknowledge the reality of the circumstance. It can put us back in control of our thoughts, emotions, and reactions. When we stop fighting, there is a sense of inner calm and stability, allowing us to approach the situation with a clear and open mind.

The goal is to tap into our inner reserves of strength and resilience, which is easier when we let go of the constant struggle of fighting against reality. Acceptance allows us to focus on what we *can* control and take action to improve our situation.

But when we go a step further past acceptance into *embracing* the challenge, we no longer see the situation as a problem at all. We view it as an opportunity.

Looking for Clues

While it isn't always a cinch to instantly embrace an unexpected interruption, the goal is to shift from seeing the situation as daunting to feeling it is manageable, then shift further to recognizing it is actually positive.

Ready to take your first step in embracing life's curveballs? Visit www.actuallyicanbook.com *to download the Embrace & Grow worksheet—your guide to turning challenges into triumphs.*

EMBRACING THE "AND"

I took for granted the simple fact that I could visit the oncology center *with my husband*. How would I know that just two months later, visitors would not be allowed in any hospital or clinic?

Rob and I found ourselves ushered into one of Dr. Horkheimer's diminutive examination rooms. Two nondescript chairs lined the wall, their upholstery a bit faded from years of patients coming and going. The walls, painted a soft, clinical shade of white, held no artwork or distractions, save for a small mirror (because, of course, we'd want to check our makeup as we waited for the oncologist).

In the other corner stood the typical examination table. It had that familiar roll of disposable white paper neatly pulled across the top, seeming to crinkle every time I looked at it. An adjustable rolling stool, with its worn-out wheels, rested near a sink, waiting for Dr. Horkheimer to make his entrance.

These rooms, designed for functionality over comfort, had a sterile ambiance.

Luckily, that was contrasted starkly with the doctor's warm, comforting nature. Remember, this was the man who had said, "We're not going to treat this cancer. We're going to *cure* it."

Although the weight of anticipation grew with each passing second, the mood immediately shifted as Dr. Horkheimer came in, sat down on the stool, and began to chart the course for our next steps.

I had heard that after a mastectomy, breast cancer treatment could involve radiation, chemotherapy, or hormone-blocking medicine. I braced myself for the doctor's prognosis.

I felt a knot tighten in my stomach when I heard his verdict. I would endure all of it. Chemo, radiation, *and* a decade of hormone-blocking pills. I won the trifecta!

The absurdity of my situation washed over me. The entire trajectory of my diagnosis still felt surreal. I wasn't even sick! One moment, I was soaring high, feeling invincible. The next, I discovered a tiny, inconvenient but easy-to-remove cancer dot. And now, it seemed, I was facing the Goliath of treatments.

As the doctor detailed the plan, an interesting thought crossed my mind. You see, I've never been an "either/or" kind of gal. I've always chosen a more abundant mindset. Why settle for one when you can have both, right? When presented with a buffet, I'd always been one to sample everything.

It appeared that I was being offered a full smorgasbord. I'd best bring my appetite.

I've always preached that you don't have to be an "either / or" person. In many situations, why not choose both? 😕

So it seems very fitting that when I got my reports that would tell me if I needed further treatment (radiation OR chemo OR hormone inhibitors), the answer would be... ALL.

Dr. Horkheimer presented three possible chemotherapy intensities: light, medium, and the most intensive. The tougher the treatment, the more likely it would complete its intended purpose—to kill any remaining cancer cells. And, of course, the more ruthless the side effects would be.

Because I was young and healthy (was there a hint of irony in his voice?), he believed I could handle the maximum level. We were going all in.

That meant sixteen sessions spread across five grueling months. Yes, I would lose my hair. And although the doctor refrained from detailing any other potential side effects (he believed in letting patients face the challenge without any preconceived notions), there was a silent acknowledgment—it would be tough.

I could sense Rob's concern growing with each revelation, his grip on my hand tightening ever so slightly. He's always been my anchor, and in that moment, his protective instincts were palpable.

The timeframe was set. Three weeks later, chemo would commence. I had to arrange a screening and schedule a procedure to implant a chemo "port" in my upper chest. This device would serve as a gateway to my body. Doctors and nurses could access this port to draw blood and administer chemo drugs. While cumbersome and invasive, it would eliminate the need to search for and access my veins during every visit and for every treatment.

The wheels were in motion, and preparation was underway.

Exiting the clinic, a blend of determination, intrigue, and anticipation coursed through me. The next phase loomed on the horizon, and it promised to be one heck of a ride.

I CAN'T PLAN BOOBS, SO LET'S PLAN HAIR

Nika Stewart ✔
January 26, 2020 · 🌐

Why is every ad in my Facebook feed for bras? 😶
Better question: Why am I clicking them all and looking at them?

Since we couldn't replace my expanders until chemotherapy and radiation were complete, my perfect-boob plans were put on hold. So, why not shift gears and focus on my mane? After all, if I wasn't about to sport a brand-new set of implants, I could certainly flaunt a fresh new hairstyle!

For a few weeks, anyway.

My locks were predicted to start vacating about two weeks after the first chemo session. This meant the clock was ticking, and I had precisely five weeks to dream up a fabulous transformation, put the plan into action, and enjoy my new look.

There was a big part of me that had always been envious of women rocking those short, fierce 'dos. I had hidden behind my long tresses for so long. This was a golden opportunity to act brave.

So, where does a gal go for hairspiration? Social media to the rescue!

I threw out a challenge.

I am looking for a cute, sassy, short cut to try right away.
Got any fun examples to share with me? Gonna choose one
very soon. (all wild, colorful, zany looks encouraged)

In essence, I was saying, "Watch this space. I'm about to go bold!"

My inbox was flooded! Pics, links, wild color suggestions— you name it.

But among the sea of responses, an unexpected suggestion stood out: a wig crafted from my own hair. The catch? I'd need to hack it off in sections, right down to the scalp, leaving behind a patchy, buzzed battlefield (albeit for a short time before it all fell out).

Now, while the idea of wearing "me" on a bald day felt comforting, I'd miss out on my brief stint as the short-hair sassy diva. It was a hair-teasing dilemma!

I did a bit of dithering, feeling conflicted and unsure.

The Joy of Tress Management: Creative Outlets

Okay, bear with me for a moment. While my world was swirling with medical tests and the not-so-subtle hum of anxiety, there I sat, consumed by my crowning glory. Yep, my hair. In the grand scheme of things, one might wonder, *Seriously? With all that's happening, she's worried about her hair?*

Absolutely. And here's why.

It's important to realize that in the face of overwhelming life events, it's natural for our minds to seek respite. It's like we're hardwired to find these pockets of diversion when our worries momentarily get parked outside, and we have a mini mental vacation.

During this time, my hair dilemma became that pocket—my own creative outlet. But it wasn't really about the hair. It was about the freedom to obsess over something trivial, lighthearted, and maybe a bit whimsical amidst the cancer chaos.

Creative outlets aren't mere escapes. They're gateways to magical realms where our mind is allowed to breathe.

Let's talk about the therapeutic nature of these outlets. Tapping into that creative spark transforms how we cope with challenges. Through them, we experience an increased sense of mindfulness, a decline in anxiety, and a notable happiness spike.

A happiness spike!

It's as if these creative ventures give us a sandbox to play in, with giant barriers keeping out the scary concerns.

For someone dealing with adversity, the benefits go even deeper.

Diving into creative activities reveals parts of ourselves we might've overlooked. Confidence increases when we realize we've made a choice that reflects who we are. We become more innovative, creating pathways in our minds that help us adapt, evolve, and find new ways to cope.

Then there's that magical thing called flow. You know that state where you're so engrossed in what you're doing that the world fades away? That's not just joyful, it's healing. It's a temporary oasis, a safe space where worries don't touch you.

So, my seemingly frivolous obsession with haircuts was more than a fun diversion. It was my anchor, my little realm of control in a sea of unpredictability. This outlet reminded me that amidst the intense whirlwind of life, there's always room for play, passion, and creativity.

And let's not overlook the fact that for many of us, our hair is a central component of our appearances and, in effect, our self-esteem. Try to imagine for a moment how you would feel if faced with the imminent reality of losing your hair.

Would this news roll off your shoulders (as my hair was about to do)? For many, this development would lead to considerable consternation. After all, the hair-loss-prevention industry continues to thrive, as people—both men and women—go to great lengths (pun intended) to rescue their receding hairlines.

So, while my illness had much more serious implications than merely losing my hair, I nonetheless felt my impending baldness deserved attention as well. Besides, this was one of the less serious chapters of my journey that I could turn into a bit of entertainment for myself and use as a creative outlet.

I embraced those unexpected outlets: hairstyles, scalp painting, writing music, TikTok. (Oh, we'll get to TikTok in a bit).

On my hardest days, these creative passions gave me strength.

Embrace your own creative outlets. Get the SHINE Creative Escape Toolkit at www.actuallyicanbook.com *for ideas and prompts to unlock your creative potential.*

RIGHTING MY STORY

"Sticks and stones may break your bones, but words can break your spirit." – Nika Stewart

Best-selling author and life and business strategist Tony Robbins says that the simplest tool for immediately transforming the quality of our lives is changing our words.

Great leaders use words to empower teams, command respect, and change hearts and minds.

But what about using our words *internally* to transform our own stories?

Back to my hair-raising decision . . .

Make a wig from my hair?

Get a short haircut?

I went back and forth for a day or so . . . then decided to chop it off.

I excitedly scheduled an appointment at a local salon where a Jen, a good friend of mine, worked, and with even more excitement, I *drove* to the appointment. I hadn't been able to use my arms to drive a car since my operation a few weeks earlier.

The sensation of freedom surged through me as I revved up my car's engine. It was a reclaiming of a bit of control. Amazing how we take these small abilities for granted, isn't it?

Freedom is... being able to drive after 3 weeks.

You might think that my haircut was the big event of that day. But something else happened that almost made me forget about my new 'do.

As I got back in my car after my haircut (and after spending a few minutes admiring myself in the rearview mirror), I looked up and saw I was parked in front of a Dunkin' Donuts. I sat for a minute, debating what I wanted. A coffee? A breakfast sandwich?

As I sat thinking, my phone rang. It was Jimmy from the financial department of the cancer treatment center.

"I'm calling to go over the costs of your upcoming chemotherapy treatments. The first treatment will be $7,842.68. Will you be okay covering that?"

Will I be okay covering that? I was confused. I had insurance. Obviously, my out-of-pocket cost was going to be less.

"I'm okay with that," I said, "but I have insurance."

"Yes," he said, "and according to your insurance, your obligation for the first treatment will be $7,842.68. The actual cost is double."

"Oh. So, you're saying I will have to pay about eight thousand dollars for my chemotherapy?"

"For the first treatment, yes."

More confusion.

He continued. "The second treatment will cost you $4,628.42."

He went on to tell me about the cost of each of my sixteen upcoming treatments. The total I would owe, he told me, was about $100,000.

"What?!?!"

One-hundred-thousand dollars was *my* responsibility. And this was just for the chemotherapy. I then had several more treatment regimens to complete.

"Wait," I said. "I have insurance. I have insurance for exactly this type of situation. I know this is going to cost money. But once I reach my maximum out-of-pocket expense, the insurance will cover everything. Once I pay out $8,500, the rest is paid to you by my insurance company."

"No, I've looked at your insurance, and once you've reached your maximum out-of-pocket cost, they will only pay for 50% of drugs and the administration of those drugs. That's what chemotherapy is. Chemo drugs and the administration of them. The cost is about $200,000."

"So, after I pay my 'maximum' of $8,500, my insurance will only cover 50% of that cost?"

"Yes."

"But isn't that what an out-of-pocket maximum is? The maximum amount I will have to pay out of my pocket? It's right there in the phrase itself—'out-of-pocket maximum.'"

It seemed as though the insurance companies and healthcare industry would have to work on updating their terminology. Apparently, this "maximum" was actually an "arbitrary, approximate, meaningless, maximum-unless-something-else-is-needed" estimate. It made no sense whatsoever.

I hung up and called my husband in a panic.

Although I thought this would set his brain afire, he acted calm. He told me not to worry. We would be okay. He is my hero.

But we now had an unexpected $100,000 bill to deal with.

I looked up again at the Dunkin' and decided not to go in. I worried about spending two dollars on a cup of coffee.

A few blocks from home, the phone rang again. It was Jimmy.

"I have to make a tiny clarification," he said.

My heart dropped even further. What else?

"After you pay your maximum out-of-pocket, the insurance does not pay 50% of drugs and the administration of drugs. They pay 100%."

Huh?

"I'm sorry," I said to Jimmy. "Can you repeat that? You said you had a tiny clarification, and that sounds like a $91,500 clarification."

He repeated himself, acting as if this tiny, insignificant error on his part was just a silly little mix-up that didn't make much difference.

"So, you're saying that after I pay out $8,500, I am no longer responsible for paying any more?"

"That's right," he told me.

I made him repeat it three more times to make sure I heard him correctly.

When I got home, I ran into the house and yelled to my husband, "We just made $91,500!"

~~~

We are the authors of our lives, not just the main characters. We have the power to choose our own narratives. That means we can describe our journeys in a way that empowers us, adds joy, makes our lives better—even if the circumstances traditionally call for negative descriptions.

Changing our inner dialogue can help us break through self-imposed limitations, create new goals, and live a more fulfilling life.

If the plot feels wrong, it's time to "right" a new story.

When I publicly shared the story of how I earned $91.500, I wasn't just painting a picture for the world; I was sketching out a roadmap for my psyche.

As I journeyed through cancer and its many challenges, I had a profound realization about the stories we tell ourselves. It confirmed just how influential our words are in shaping our perceptions of reality.

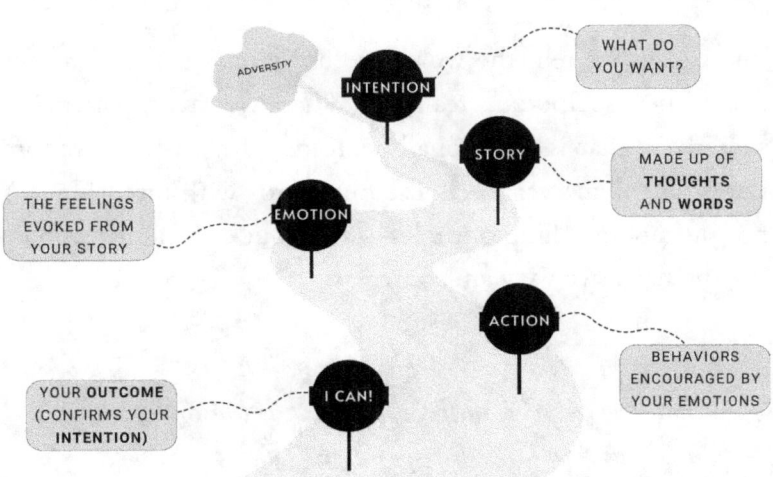

ACTUALLY I CAN
THE DELIBERATE PATH TO CONQUERING ADVERSTY

Every time we vocalize our thoughts or post something online, we're adding a stitch to the tapestry of our life's narrative. It's no secret that today's digital age can amplify specific outlooks. For instance, when a term goes viral on social media, it can swiftly become the dominant narrative, pushing other perspectives to the sidelines.

This continuous echo of words and ideas can trick our brains. There's a sneaky phenomenon called the "illusory truth effect." In essence, if we hear or say something often enough, our minds might start to accept it as gospel—even if it's not accurate.

If we're not vigilant, this little quirk in our cognition can subconsciously manipulate us in negative ways.

But we have the ability to deliberately choose our words and manipulate ourselves in *positive* ways.

The stories we tell, the words we use, don't just narrate our lives. They sculpt our realities. When we are experiencing something that is traditionally considered negative, it's more important than ever to choose our words with intention. It's not just about telling our tales—it's about consciously choosing the narrative we want to live by.

Ready to re-right your narrative?
Grab your Story Shift workbook, filled with exercises
to help you transform your perspective and your experience.
www.actuallyicanbook.com

LOCKS AND DOCS: GEARING UP FOR THE ROAD AHEAD

Having averted the financial crisis, it was time to prepare my body for the next five months of chemotherapy.

With my freshly snipped tresses and newfound mobility, I felt an adrenaline rush as I powered through business meetings to wrap up projects and get my team ready to step in for when I needed time off.

During one group meeting, a nurse arrived at my office door to take a blood test. I stepped into another room, rolled up my sleeve, and watched her take the sample. Then I went back to my meeting, as if this were a regular occurrence.

I was trying my best to live my life and run my business and take care of my daughter as if not much had changed.

How strange that we continue with life as normal, even when a substantial change looms. When I was nine months (and a few days) pregnant and the arrival of my daughter was imminent, I still carried on with my life as I had always done, knowing, but seemingly oblivious to the fact that at any day or any moment my day-to-day routine would be turned upside down.

As I moved toward the start of chemo, I followed my normal schedule, plugging away as I have always done.

Until one day . . .

Nika Stewart
February 2, 2020 · 🌐

Since I'm documenting my journey, I decided I should be honest - since most (all?) of my posts have been optimistic and bright. No, I'm not an in-denial Pollyanna. I have ups and downs.

This evening feels sad. Today I had to choose between 2 conflicting meetings for this week. One felt very important to my business, and the other felt very important for my health. I chose to cancel the business meeting. I know that's the right thing. And yet I still feel sad.

And very tired. I should go to sleep. But first I have to watch a few more hours of commercials. What's your fave so far?

This evening feels sad. Today I had to choose between 2 conflicting meetings for this week. One felt very important to my business, and the other felt very important for my health. I chose to cancel the business meeting. I know that's the right thing. And yet I still feel sad.

Since I was taking my audience along on my adventure, I wanted to share the ups and the downs. And it's a great thing I did.

The comments on my post were as expected. My friends poured out their encouragement. "Your health comes first!" they all said.

But the very next day I got a text from my doctor.

She had seen my post!

"Were you talking about our appointment? I can meet another time. Don't cancel your business meeting."

In that moment, I realized that sharing your journey can be even more powerful than I had assumed. Yes, people might be inspired when you're honest about your struggles, but they might also surprise you with just how much assistance they have to offer.

The blessings of social media kept coming. With every post I made, I witnessed the vast reach and power of this digital age we live in. It wasn't just about staying updated or sharing photos anymore; social media had become a place for genuine connections and unexpected support.

Sharing my updates and engaging on social media turned out to be one of the most enriching parts of my journey. It was a testament to the genuine connections we can foster, even in a world dominated by screens.

Nika Stewart
February 3, 2020 · 🌐

Follow Up to yesterday's post, where I told you I had to choose between 2 conflicting meetings (one for my business & one for my health).

My doctor saw my post and texted me to ask if I wanted to change the appointment so I didn't have to cancel my business meeting. 😊

The blessings keep coming.

Thank you Dr. Jessica! (and thank you, Facebook 😊)

Follow Up to yesterday's post, where I told you I had to choose between 2 conflicting meetings (one for my business & one for my health). My doctor saw my post and texted me to ask if I wanted to change the appointment so I didn't have to cancel my business meeting. 😊

The blessings keep coming.
Thank you Dr. Jessica! (and thank you, Facebook)

As I kept sharing snippets of my journey—the highs, the lows, and the in-betweens—what surprised me the most was the ripple effect they had. Other women started reaching out, sharing their stories, their fears, and their victories. Some contacted me just to say how much my updates meant to them, offering their support in return. It was as if we were all holding each other's hands through the internet clouds.

If you're inspired to share your own story, head over to www.actuallyicanbook.com for a guide on navigating social media with authenticity and vulnerability. Find advice and templates to help you share your challenges powerfully and positively.

PORT OF CALL:
ANOTHER SURGICAL STOPOVER

Things seemed to be moving along smoothly, but before my chemo journey could officially begin, I had to make another pit stop at the hospital for the installation of a chemo port on the upper right side of my chest.

This might seem like another procedural annoyance, but for me, it heralded a semblance of relief. After the lymph node removal during the mastectomy, every needle prick became a dreaded affair. A poke of my right arm carried the potential of irreversible lymphedema, a condition that creates dangerous swelling caused by the removal of clusters of lymph nodes in my right arm. And the left arm? Those veins were persistently on vacation. Attempts to take blood were taking four to six jabs, and I often felt exhausted, annoyed, and depleted.

The port, however, promised to change that.

With a port, healthcare workers would have a direct line of access. No more playing pin-the-needle on my veins. Drawing blood, administering fluids, or injecting chemo medications would be much quicker and easier.

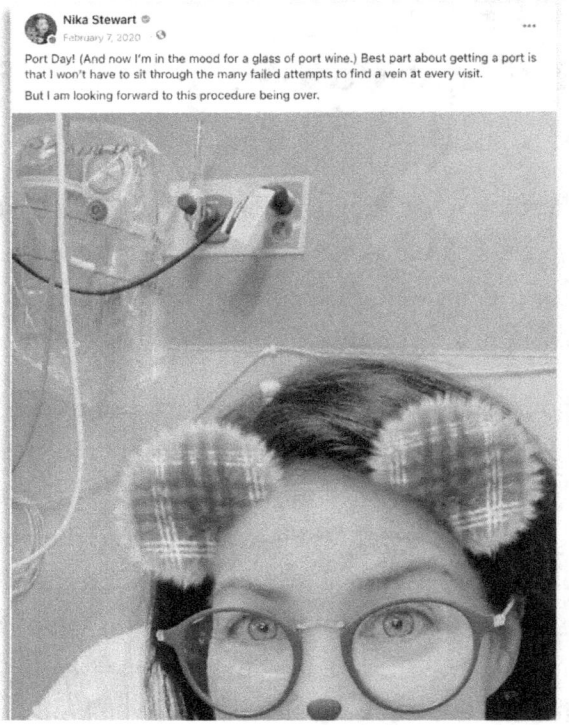

Port Day! (And now I'm in the mood for a glass of port wine.) Best part about getting a port is that I won't have to sit through the many failed attempts to find a vein at every visit.

But I am looking forward to this procedure being over.

The hospital waiting room was abuzz with activity as I settled in. A nearby TV murmured with the day's headlines, which under normal circumstances I might've tuned out. But today, one particular news bulletin snagged my attention.

A man, fresh off a cruise ship docking in New York, had tested positive for Covid-19.

New York—practically my neighbor!

A shiver ran down my spine as I considered the ramifications. The images from other countries showed empty streets, closed shops, and communities supporting each other by singing songs through apartment windows as they holed up inside.

Entire nations were in lockdown, their citizens confined to their homes. Were we on the brink of that dystopian reality? The mere thought felt daunting. The virus, previously just a distant shadow on the horizon, now seemed real—and imminent.

The situation was surreal; an impending threat that felt both near and distant, conceivable yet somehow unimaginable.

But while the world was becoming obsessed with the possibility of a global pandemic, I needed to focus on my current situation.

The prep area was bright and sterile, with many curtained sections. I heard anxious patients and supportive partners chatting with the nurses, and I realized that many people were having a much harder time than I was. Rob was by my side, continuously squeezing my hand with a reassuring grip. I certainly don't like surgeries, but I think he was more nervous than I was.

Tina, the nurse, wearing traditional scrubs and a gentle smile, began her standard pre-procedure checklist. It was a routine she'd clearly performed countless times. She ran through the list briskly.

Then she got to the question that left me flummoxed.

"Do you drink alcohol?"

"Um," I hesitated. How do I answer this accurately?

That question seemed so black and white. Shouldn't there be a scale? A spectrum?

I mused internally. If I toast a glass of champagne on New Year's Eve, technically, I'd have to answer "yes." Likewise, if I became best friends with a bottle of tequila every evening, my answer would still be "yes."

The span between those extremes felt like equating a water droplet to an ocean when asked "Is the area wet?"

Finally, I responded affirmatively, laughing and saying that they should make a change in their questionnaire.

Tina agreed, and we had a chuckle.

But my jovial mood was quickly disrupted.

It was time to insert the needle for anesthesia.

Recalling previous traumatic experiences, I firmly stated, "I want your best for this. My left arm veins are quite shy."

The nurse looked confident. "Don't worry, I've been doing this for years." Another nurse nearby echoed the same confidence. "Nothing to worry about—you're in great hands with Tina. She's the best stick in the department!"

Uh-oh. Was Tina of the same legendary status as Donna? I closed my eyes and hoped for the best.

After three frustrating and excruciating attempts that felt like fire coursing through my arm, it became clear that even her years of experience had met their match in my obdurate vasculature.

"Let's get the expert," she said cheerfully, as if it was a brilliant, helpful idea she just thought up.

As I waited, a mix of nausea and annoyance filled me.

A patient should expect precision, attention to detail, meticulous care . . . in prep questions and in needlework.

With the thin tube snugly nestled in place, I breathed a sigh of relief. I said goodbye to Rob as they wheeled me into the OR.

And, oh boy, the cocktail of medications they infused me with felt like I was floating on a cloud made of marshmallows. Unicorns probably feel just like this after a long, magical day of galloping through rainbows. This was the most delightful rest I had had for as long as I could remember. I wondered if I could bottle up that feeling and take a sip whenever I needed.

But alas, a gentle tap brought me back from my whimsical wanderings. And I saw a strangely shaped lump sticking out of my right clavicle, the newest companion to join me on my travels.

Excitement, wonder, anger, and Chuck (my port).

Yes, I named my port Chuck. Because Chuck is a nickname for Charles.

Get it? (IYKYK—*General Hospital* fans will understand.)

With Chuck, I felt equipped and ready to face the next chapter of my healing journey.

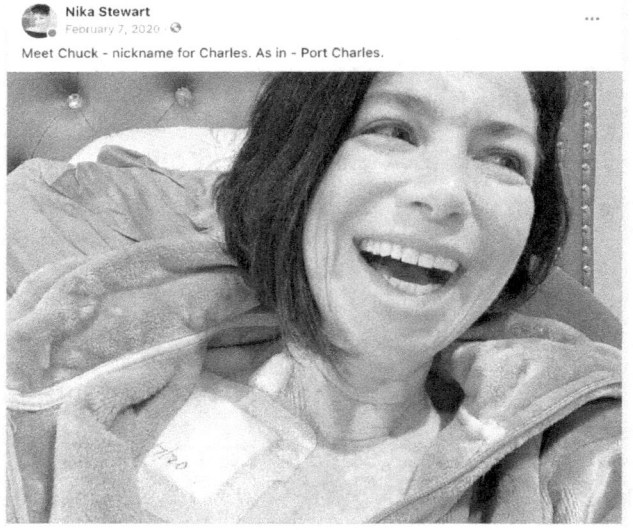

Meet Chuck – nickname for Charles. As in – Port Charles.

CHEM-HUH?-THERAPY

There's something undeniably ominous about the word "che-motherapy," the way it's whispered in conversations, usually followed by a sad, sympathetic nod. It's a term that is both so ubiquitous in our culture and yet so remote. You hear about it, read about it, perhaps even know someone who's gone through it. But surely, it's something that happens to *other* people, something in those tear-jerker movies or touching memoirs.

I was about to embark on a five-month journey, and even as the starting line approached, it felt more like I was acting in a movie of someone else's life than living my own. During every procedure, every appointment, every result, I felt as if I were pretending, filling in for someone else, going through the mo-tions but not really being there.

There was a disconnect. I mean, I was eating Nutella with my daughter, singing with my band, and working with new, amazingly interesting clients. How could I fit into this scary medical world of chemotherapy?

One morning, still nestled under my cozy blanket, I pulled out my phone to write a Facebook post.

That's when the realization struck me. I was writing about the challenges faced by people braving the cancer journey, the lit-tle indignities, the surreal procedures, and the highs and lows. But I was writing *as if I were an outsider* peeking in through a window, not someone about to open the door and step inside.

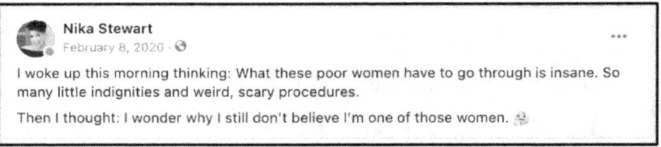

I woke up this morning thinking: What these poor women have to go through is insane. So many little indignities and weird, scary procedures.

Then I thought: I wonder why I still don't believe I'm one of those women. 😊

Why did I feel like I was chronicling someone else's journey?

Maybe it was a defense mechanism, a mental buffer to protect myself. Or maybe I had subconsciously decided that if this was my journey, my story, I would write it in my own words, with my own voice.

I wasn't going to go through this like everyone else.

Nika Stewart
February 10, 2020 · 🌐

Workday's done, and I need some kitty snuggling time as I try to relax and make a list of all the reasons I'm looking forward to tomorrow (chemo day one)...

1. A few hours of tech-free relaxation (okay, maybe not totally tech-free. I may feel like snapchatting 😜)
2. Getting in a few hours of book reading
3. A new experience - learning what this is like, experiencing all the feelings, sensations, side effects - so maybe I can help ease someone else's fears in the future?
4. One session closer to being done

Anything else I should be focusing on? ✍️

Workday's done, and I need some kitty snuggling time as I try to relax and make a list of all the reasons I'm looking forward to tomorrow (chemo day one)...

1. A few hours of tech-free relaxation (okay, maybe not totally tech-free. I may feel like snapchatting 😄)
2. Getting in a few hours of book reading
3. A new experience - learning what this is like, experiencing all the feelings, sensations, side effects - so maybe I can help ease someone else's fears in the future?
4. One session closer to being done

Anything else I should be focusing on?

DANCING WITH THE (RED) DEVIL

I was amped up, ready for my five months of treatment to commence. Rob, of course, was accompanying me on my first treatment. But to continue the surprises I was getting throughout this journey, another curveball hit us.

Rob woke up with what we thought might be a cold. Not willing to risk the health of the immunocompromised people in the cancer center, he recused himself, and mom—my backup pillar of strength—picked me up and drove me to the chemo center.

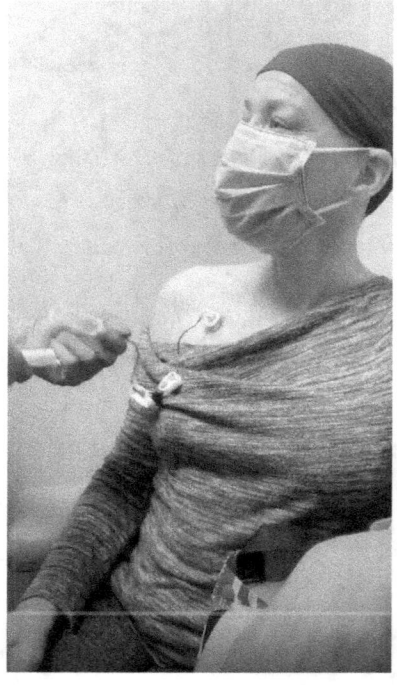

I've learned that when people think of "chemo," there is a lot of confusion about the treatment. I was the same way before I started the process. Many of my friends and my social media followers asked me a lot of questions.

"Does it hurt?"
"Is it an injection?"
"Is it like radiation?"
"Is it something you drink?"

If you or your family have never been exposed to cancer, you probably have a lot of questions about chemotherapy. As I went through my treatments, I found that many of my social media posts and pictures I shared helped to shine a light on the process.

To see this video and more, go to
www.actuallyicanbook.com

I was introduced to the large treatment room, decorated with a dozen medical recliner chairs along the perimeter. I opted for a chair tucked in the corner.

As we settled in and the medications flowed into my port, I mapped out the coming weeks in my head. I imagined friends rotating in and out, each bringing their own energy and distraction to my sessions. I planned out five months of giggles, stories, and card games, a schedule that provided not just medical support but emotional sustenance.

I even plotted a future session where Ellie would play hooky and we'd make a day of it at the chemo center. Quite an unusual mother-daughter day out!

I intended to make this journey as fun as possible.

Of course, I hadn't foreseen the looming shadow of Covid. In mere weeks, the world was going to change, and my chemo center's bustling companion room would stand eerily empty.

On that first day, though, with my mom beside me, I held onto the beauty and comfort of support and love.

As we chatted over a cookie, mom shared her idea of creating a countdown calendar. As each session completed, we could cross it off, like ticking off days to a much-awaited holiday. What a wonderful distraction, a creative outlet, and a beacon during my journey. That conversation sparked an idea, one that soon snowballed into my TikTok obsession.

But first, the Red Devil.

Oh, the Red Devil. I had heard people talking about it ominously but didn't know what to expect. It was the nickname given to a rather potent form of chemotherapy, and my schedule included four of these sessions, administered two weeks apart to give my body (and mind!) a chance to recover.

Adriamycin, or as I soon intimately knew it, the "Red Devil," looked disarmingly like neon red Kool-Aid. But this was no child's play.

After four bags of pre-medicines had dripped into my veins, it was time for the actual chemotherapy drug. The nurse walked over, not with the usual infusion bag, but with a syringe the size of a small spaceship. Seriously, I had no idea they made syringes this large. It looked like a joke, like they created this for a Broadway show about a giant who needed to receive a vaccine.

Louise, my affable nurse, explained that the Red Devil had to be pushed into the port by hand. She attached the end of the syringe to the tube flowing into my port and began to depress the plunger.

As she administered it, I sucked on ice chips, attempting to stave off painful mouth sores (a fun side effect of this chemo cocktail).

Watching as Louise thrust that red liquid into me with great force seemed eerie. It felt so strange, and chomping on ice for so long was painful and uncomfortable.

Seven minutes later, the syringe emptied, and I let out a sigh of relief.

Unfortunately, my relief was premature. She produced Syringe Number Two.

And we had to do it all over again.

That initial session felt like an unending marathon of strangeness. Between the tests, the pre-meds, the swapping of infusion bags, and the surprising double tango with the Red Devil, a surreal unease settled over me. Could I actually do this?

Over the next few days, the side effects that hit me felt like an unrelenting bout of the most bizarre flu I've ever encountered—but grotesquely magnified. It wasn't just the unyielding, low-grade nausea, but an array of ridiculous aches and oddities in my body. My bones felt heavy and achy. Every cell in me felt off-kilter, as if they were all racing in different directions, desperately trying to rip from my insides.

And then there was the indefinable weirdness, an overall sensation so peculiar it defied description. It wasn't like any illness I'd ever experienced.

Nika Stewart
February 18, 2020 · 🌐

I was duped!

My absolute knowledge that everything would be okay... The relative ease of healing after surgery... The fact that I can deal pretty well with physical pain... The supportive messages encouraging me and cheering me on...

All of these things fooled me into thinking that I would sail through this year of treatment.

And then chemo started.

And I learned I was wrong. This isn't going to be a piece of cake. But the good news?

One down! Just 15 more to go 😐

I was duped!

My absolute knowledge that everything would be okay... The relative ease of healing after surgery... The fact that I can deal pretty well with physical pain... The supportive messages encouraging me and cheering me on...

All of these things fooled me into thinking that I would sail through this year of treatment.

And then chemo started.

And I learned I was wrong. This isn't going to be a piece of cake. But the good news?

One down! Just 15 more to go 😋

How could I endure this for five months? I honestly wasn't sure I could. That week was my darkest hour.

Without any choice, I gave in to the sickness. I felt sad. I felt hopeless. I felt scared.

Then I learned something that gave me hope.

RATING THE WRETCHEDNESS

A week after my inaugural session with the Red Devil, I made my way to Dr. Horkheimer's office for a check-in. My spirit felt as battered as my body.

Trying to smile, I admitted to him, "I don't know how I'm going to endure this for five months."

He looked at me sympathetically and dropped a revelation that changed everything.

"Oh, you won't feel this bad for five months. You're only getting the Red Devil three more times over the next six weeks," he said. "Then we change to Taxol."

I knew Taxol was next in line after the initial four treatments, but it was still chemotherapy. How could it be any less grueling?

The Red Devil, he said, had the toughest side effects.

"Most people would rate the awfulness of the Red Devil as a nine or ten out of ten. But Taxol feels more like a . . ."

Time seemed to pause. My heart raced, clinging to a fragile hope.

Could Taxol provide the respite I so deeply yearned for? I dared to envision it.

Perhaps Taxol was a manageable seven, or maybe, just maybe, it was as low as a six?

I felt my heart take a breath with me . . . waiting. The small room, accentuated by the sterile paper covering the treatment bed and that lone mirror hanging on the wall, felt suddenly both suffocating and vast.

Anticipation pressed down on me. My mind raced, every fiber of my being silently imploring, pleading with a fervor I hadn't known I possessed.

Please let it be a six. Just utter that number. *Just say six.*

". . . about a one or two."

Oh. My. God.

Indescribable relief washed over me. Just three more battles with the ruthless Red Devil. That, I believed, I could withstand.

And while the next three treatments promised to be increasingly taxing, as the side effects were cumulative, Dr. Horkheimer mentioned a silver lining.

He said many patients reported feeling marginally better during their fourth treatment.

But how could that be? If each of the four treatments built on each other, adding more of the nasty drug into your body, wouldn't anyone feel even worse after the fourth infusion?

There wasn't a medical reason for this, he said. It can be attributed to the human spirit, drawing strength from the knowledge that it was the final rendezvous with the Red Devil.

It made me thankful that the treatment started with the most intensive drug first. If I started with Taxol, I might have thought that was a ten on the discomfort scale, and then would have been bulldozed by the Red Devil.

Armed with this new perspective, I reminded myself that I wasn't a passenger on this tumultuous journey, but the pilot. The Red Devil might've shaken me, but the knowledge of what awaited infused me with renewed strength.

Every bout of nausea, every moment of pain, every hair that fell from my scalp gave me another chance to dance in the rain. It wasn't about enduring this part of the journey, but about truly thriving, embracing the absurdities, finding the beautiful moments, and, most importantly, transforming every whimper into a beacon of inspiration.

With renewed optimism, it was time to look for silver linings, find things to laugh at, and turn whine into *shine*.

GRATITUDE IN THE DARKNESS

Remember Adventure, my steadfast companion on this journey? Along the way, she was momentarily overshadowed by the fleeting visitors Anger, Confusion, and Hopelessness. Yet, Adventure remained unwavering by my side. And soon, another companion emerged to walk this path with us—Gratitude.

It's natural to be grateful for life's blessings—joyous moments shared with loved ones, a warm cup of coffee, the support of a friend.

These are the easy blessings to feel grateful for. But in the aftermath of my first brush with the Red Devil, I challenged myself to find gratitude, not in the easily recognizable joys, but in the adversity itself. It's counterintuitive, isn't it?

My groans of discomfort remained undeniable realities. Yet, as I searched for relief, a realization emerged. This adversity had granted me something special.

Time.

Time to focus on myself, to prioritize my well-being, to truly delve into self-care in a way I'd never permitted myself to do before.

How often do we, in the hustle and bustle of our daily routines, genuinely prioritize ourselves? Rarely, if ever. Now, here

I was, given an enforced pause.

With the overwhelming sickness, I had no choice but to take the time to heal. And the beauty of this realization? It transformed everything.

Of course, the journey still held its challenges, but armed with Gratitude, the path seemed clearer. Every dark cloud had its silver lining. The looming five months, once a terrifying ordeal, began to feel like a gift. A gift of time, self-reflection, and above all, gratitude. Because gratitude, as I discovered, isn't just for the good days. It's the light that guides us through our darkest nights.

If you'd like to find things to be grateful for even in difficult times, grab our Gratitude Amplifier Toolkit at www.actuallyicanbook.com

LOSING LOCKS, GAINING GIGGLES

And this is where my story turns from a drama into a comedy.

Until this point, I'd been offering raw glimpses into my scary journey, sprinkling it with optimism, joy, and a good measure of humor.

Yet, as strands of hair began to litter my pillow (and my clothing, the dinner table, my laptop), a new sense of purpose emerged. I became determined to find the hilarity in every moment, especially those typically cloaked in sadness.

I started noticing the absurd, the unexpected, and the downright ridiculous. As I shared these comedic snippets online, I unknowingly created a new therapeutic outlet that would not only help me sail through this difficult part of my journey but also inspire millions of others.

Without dismissing the intensity and seriousness of the journey, I found solace in humor. It became a way to not only cope but also to connect, to show others that even in the darkest tunnels, there's room for a chuckle or two.

They say laughter is the best medicine, so I self-prescribed a heavy dose.

I'd been given a heads-up. "Fourteen days after your first chemo, expect hair loss."

Nobody mentioned the precision of that timeline. I expected some preliminary warning, perhaps a few strands on my pillowcase on day seven or eight as a gentle prelude. But no, the universe stuck rigidly to the script.

Day thirteen? Not a hair out of place. I couldn't find *one* strand on my pillowcase!

My hair's just not falling out!

But some cosmic chemo alarm buzzed on day fourteen, prompting my hair to begin its dramatic exodus.

Eager to bring my growing online community on this roller-coaster with me, I shared a snapshot. Me, brandishing a clump of hair with a dash of defiance and a sprinkle of amusement.

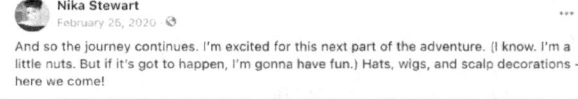

Nika Stewart
February 26, 2020

And so the journey continues. I'm excited for this next part of the adventure. (I know. I'm a little nuts. But if it's got to happen, I'm gonna have fun.) Hats, wigs, and scalp decorations - here we come!

And so the journey continues. I'm excited for this next part of the adventure. (I know. I'm a little nuts. But if it's got to happen, I'm gonna have fun.) Hats, wigs, and scalp decorations - here we come!

I eagerly laced up for the next phase of the adventure. And yep, I know that sounds nuts. But if destiny had this penciled in for me, I was going to ride it with flair. When else would I give myself permission to explore the world of hats, wigs, and edgy scalp art?

As the clock inched towards 8:30 am, and with my hair playing a vanishing act, I swathed my head in a stylish scarf. With the memory of the first chemo fresh, there was an air of déjà vu, but also an itch of anticipation. What surprises did this week hold? Especially concerning my ever-diminishing hairline.

Comfort items in tow—a snug blanket and a Wonder Woman plushie, both loving tokens from friends—I stepped into the chemo room.

A critical dilemma presented itself. Should I stick to my familiar chair or flirt with a new location each session? With Adventure, my constant companion by my side, I felt like an explorer charting different terrains. Each spot promised its own unique tale, urging me to embrace the unknown.

While pondering this life-altering decision, Rob's presence was a comforting constant. He was there, right beside me, as we geared up for round two.

Nika Stewart
February 25, 2020 · 🌐

My friend and I are ready for chemo #2.

{big thanks to Michael & Camellia for the extra comfort and warmth}

My friend and I are ready for chemo #2

(In case you were wondering, I chose a different corner chair).

The next day greeted me with a poignant reality. I was about to fully step into the shoes of a cancer patient.

Obviously, I had been playing this role for the last few months. But now the mounting tufts of hair appearing on my laptop as I tried to work were an undeniable sign of the visible transformation that lay ahead. If ever there were an iconic symbol of the cancer experience, a bald head was surely it.

This was the day I would embrace that symbol, and in doing so, deeply feel and acknowledge the role I was now living.

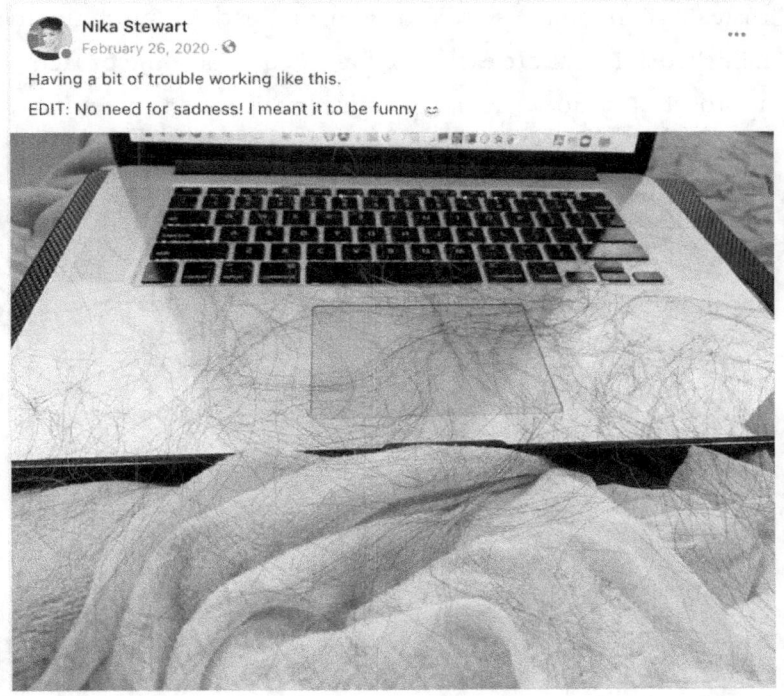

Having a bit of trouble working like this.

Edit: No need for sadness! I meant it to be funny. 😊

DANCING SHAVING IN THE RAIN

Instead of taking the slow and agonizing path of watching my hair shed a little more each day, I decided to take the proactive approach and do what many cancer patients do: preemptive baldness!

I had purchased a hair clipper specifically for this defining moment and the box sat patiently on my hall table. It seemed to beckon to me each day, as if whispering, "Is today the day? Whenever you're ready, I'm here."

Each time I glanced its way, a mix of anticipation and eagerness bubbled up within me. It wasn't just a hair clipper, it was the symbolic tool of my upcoming transformation, and I found myself growing more and more restless to wield it.

I spent hours researching the best way to shave my head. It was important to do this in the safest way. Apparently, it was crucial to not clip the hair too close. In other words, don't shave to the scalp. Leaving a smidge of hair would ensure those tiny follicles didn't end up trapped, like splinters of ingrown hair.

Ellie, ever my brave, supportive fourteen-year-old, was eager to take on the shaving duty. But I figured she could use a hand from someone who'd been in the hair game a bit longer. So I rang up my hairstylist buddy Jen, who was on board in a heartbeat, generously agreeing to swoop in with her equipment and supervise Ellie.

As I planned this iconic event for the evening, Adventure kept whispering in my ear, *Why not make the event an* event?

What if I turned my head-shaving experience into a Facebook livestream? My social media posts had been getting a significant amount of attention and engagement. Why not harness that newfound popularity and do some good? The concept of a virtual charity head-shaving party started to take shape.

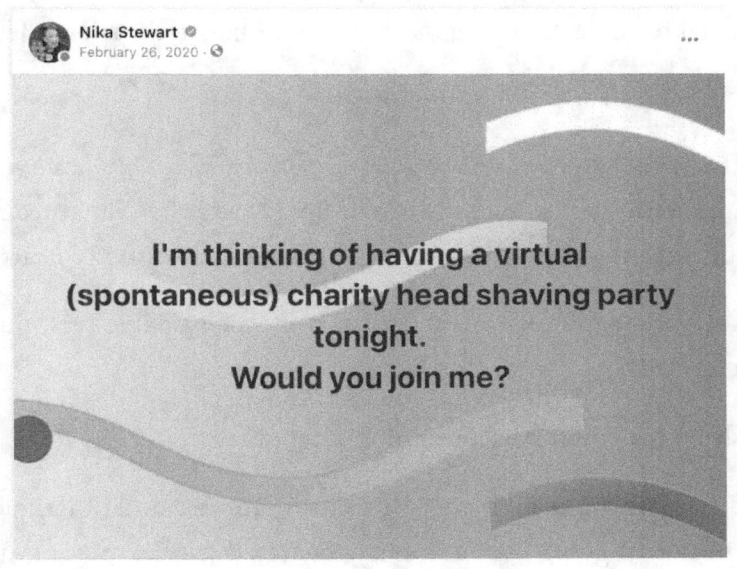

As the day rolled on and the evening approached, the anticipation grew.

Oh, my god. I was doing this. I was going to shave my head.

BUZZ! A BALDHEADED BALLET

Setting: A cozy, modern kitchen with warm overhead lights. Center stage stands a lone chair, bathed in a spotlight of anticipation. To the side, a set of hair clippers, resting like a knight's sword just before a duel.

Our stars for the evening: an anxious mom, her talented daughter Ellie, and the guiding hand of hairstylist friend, Jen.

~~~

The virtual arena is set for a grand performance. My head will take center stage, with viewers from all over the digital realm cheering and possibly donating for a cause close to my heart.

The anticipation is real, the *buzz* in the air palpable (yes, pun intended).

The event could have been monumental.

But, as the hour draws near, I feel a looming cloud of fatigue. Dreams of going live fade as my energy dwindles. Setting up the camera and lighting, creating appropriate links—it's all too much.

I try to forgive myself for this deviation from the script.

It's time for the main feature, however. I decide we will perform in private, no cameras except for a recording taken by Rob for our own documentation.

In walks Jen, with grace and expertise. The same hands that had recently given me a chic, short haircut now hold the key to the next phase of my journey. Close on her heels, Ellie, my brave co-star, buzzes with trepidation.

The electric hair trimmer purchased a few days ago gleams on the counter. I seat myself on the throne, ready for the act.

Ellie, eager and a touch nervous, holds the buzzing tool, its presence emitting a strong energy even before it comes alive. Jen, the guide, whispers advice and encouragement, ensuring every movement is purposeful and gentle.

Just before we begin, Jen asks, "Want to close your eyes?"

I respond with a defiant no.

But as the buzzer roars to life and touches my head, my eyes snap shut. The electric hum fills the room, a steady rhythm guiding Ellie's dance as she sweeps across my scalp, every movement resonating with purpose and love.

As we near completion, Jen suggests an improvisation. "Let's add a unique touch, shall we?"

With delicate precision, the word NIKA is etched onto the back of my scalp, a fun souvenir from this transformative ballet.

The dance concludes, but the memories linger.

A few months ago, doctors told me my little cancer experience would be as easy as a haircut.

This buzzing ballet is more than just a haircut. It's a statement, a rebirth, a story of resilience and transformation.

See a video of this event at www.actuallyicanbook.com

Rob walked toward me with a mirror in his hand.

"Are you ready?" he asked.

Taking a deep breath, I nodded.

He held up the mirror, and with a sense of suspense, I slowly turned toward it.

A startling new reflection stared back at me. I was filled with the expected mix of awe and disorientation as I methodically rubbed my hand over my scalp. It felt odd, the prickly stubble a sharp contrast to the silky strands that once cascaded down.

Yet, in the midst of the strangeness, a pulse of excitement surfaced, a heartbeat of anticipation to share my transformed self with the world.

I wasn't ready to post a photo yet. I wanted to sleep on it and think about how I would share my new self.

But I did send a few photos to my brother, who was way ahead of me on the head-shaving front, having decided to rid himself of his locks several years earlier.

The next morning, I woke up to this post on Facebook:

Me and my amazing, brave, kick-ass big sister started out as opposites but keep looking more and more alike…now I bet you can't guess who's who. I used to act like the tough one, but the secret is out. Don't mess with sis. #twins

RELEASING PERFECTION

A week later, my band had a gig scheduled.

After two power-packed chemo sessions, I needed permission to perform. We were going to be in a crowded place, talk of Covid was growing louder, and I wasn't sure how compromised my immune system might be.

My doc gave me the green light.

"Go rock that stage," he said. Maybe not those exact words, but that's what I heard.

There was another approval stamp I secretly yearned for, however.

Aside from chemo treatments and doctors' appointments, this was going to be the first time I left the house to be with other people. And I was not only going to be in public; I was going to be singing in front of a crowd with many eyes on me.

Queue Wigathon!

My bedroom became a wig parade—vibrant rainbows of wild hair, chic bobs, and the one that looked like my old self.

Remember my obsession with choosing a hairstyle? I had converted that creative outlet into a passion for wigs.

In my head, I pictured stepping onto the stage with a mane

of wild purple hair crashing down over my eyes, or maybe switching it up every couple of tracks for dramatic flair.

But with every wig I tried on, I felt ickier. Nothing seemed right.

Amidst the chemo side effects, I just craved some comfort.

But, more than comfort, I yearned to be true to myself.

Sure, I loved the dramatic flair of my full long hair, flipping it, swinging it, and coyly brushing it away from my eyes during performances. These were my signature moves, my rockstar edge. But the artificial hair replacements didn't capture that same feeling.

And now I was about to face an audience. Familiar faces, new ones. The thought was both thrilling and horrifying.

Talk about an important personal crisis! Here I was, battling cancer, and I'm having an internal debate about hair, or the lack thereof.

Was it vain? Hell yes. But I'm human. And this was uncharted territory for me. I had no idea how to act or who to be.

Deep down, I just wanted to be me. Authentic. Real. No disguises.

In other words, bald.

But I craved validation.

So, what did I do? Of course, I spilled my guts on Facebook.

Struggle of the Day:
(It's a big one and I need lots of support)
(Just kidding. It means nothing and I just want to whine
about not being able to make a tiny decision)

Do I show up at tonight's band gig bald(ish), or do I wear
a wig?

Every response was some version of "go bald" or "do whatever makes you feel good."

- Au natural for sure
- Go with your gut and do what feels more right for you.

And only you.

- You do what makes you happy.
- I say go natural.
- Whatever makes you feel good.
- Do what you feel like; you will rock it.

. . . and so many more messages encouraging me to do what I wanted to do.

Plus a few other fun suggestions:

- Ooooh oooh oooh wild woman face paint temporary tattoo on your scalp?
- Tiara!
- I'm feeling bald with bandana.
- Go topless, wear red lipstick, sing your heart out and own it baby!!

And the best comment was from a friend who had gone through a cancer journey with her young daughter.

"There's no right/wrong way to go through cancer—no judgment zone—you have my support all the way."

My inner voice had been supported.

I know I didn't need permission or anyone's blessing to do what I felt in my heart, but this was all so new. And the outpouring of support was so helpful.

So I showed up at the band gig without hair.

Walking in was scary. I knew I looked weird. How would my friends greet me? Would the bar patrons stare?

Obviously, my friends greeted me with open arms. And the other customers? I guess they assumed I was a rock and roll singer who shaved her head.

During a break, I visited the restroom in the bar and encountered one of the patrons applying her makeup. She saw me walk in and said, "You know, I am so in awe of you. I've always thought about shaving my head, but never had the guts to do it. I love the look!"

Imagine that! She thought I did this as a style choice! It made me feel like I was at least projecting confidence, and that my insecurities of appearing in public bald were well hidden.

The whole experience was uncomfortable. And exciting. And awkward. And exhilarating.

Carrying On with Cancer

While my main focus was dealing with my treatments, life still carried on full force. I couldn't just simply shut everything down until my regimen was complete. I needed to adjust and reintegrate myself into my daily activities, my business, and my life—bald, bold, and badass!

Although I didn't have many chances to be in public over the next few months (Covid lockdown started in my area a week later), I went to all my medical appointments bald. I attended all my Zoom business meetings bald. I hosted all my video presentations bald.

I was met with the most incredible empathy and encouragement.

I found it incredible that in the past, when I tried to present myself as a professional leader with everything put together in order to motivate others to become the best version of themselves, the response was varied and often lackluster.

But the moment I shared my imperfections—the things I was taught to hide: my physical oddities, my fears, my struggles—my message resonated in powerful ways.

I had always known that we should celebrate our uniqueness. But I never realized that the things we were ashamed of were part of that.

After I got past the initial fear of putting myself out in the world with my bald head, it became easier, for many reasons.

Yes, I had expanded my comfort zone by sharing my raw self. But now I also didn't have to think about what I needed to hide.

Covering up shame is like a lie that you must remember.

Who did I tell? What exactly did I say? What do I need to do to keep up the façade?

It's exhausting.

Exposing the truth removed all that work. And the amazing response made this choice ever better.

I had spent thousands of dollars on wigs to hide my shame before I realized I had nothing to hide.

MIRROR IMAGES

In the cozy confines of a therapist's office, a distressed mother once lamented, "I don't understand why my daughter thinks she isn't pretty. I keep telling her she is beautiful, and she truly is. Every time I look at her, I make sure she knows. But she refuses to believe it."

The therapist, leaning in with genuine curiosity, asked, "And when you look at yourself, what do you tell yourself?"

The mother hesitated. "Well. . . I don't think I'm pretty. I see all these wrinkles, I hate my hair, and I've never been happy with my body."

The therapist nodded thoughtfully. "That, right there, is why your daughter doesn't feel pretty."

Children, especially daughters, not only listen to our words but absorb our feelings, our self-perceptions. It shouldn't be a surprise when they echo our silent sentiments about ourselves.

That story is a stark reminder of the power our self-esteem wields, not just over our own perceptions, but for those who look up to us, as well. My own experience brought this lesson home in a deeply personal way.

Newly bald, I had an encounter that served as an awakening. One day, after picking up my daughter from school, I chatted with a dad through my car window. I found myself saying, almost offhandedly, "I'm not very pretty right now."

As we drove away, my daughter turned to look at me and said, "But mom, you're beautiful."

Her words stung with the force of truth. By criticizing myself so casually, I was inadvertently teaching her it was acceptable to diminish oneself.

So, while I still often did a double-take whenever I passed a mirror, I immediately made it a point to embrace the reflection staring back.

And why shouldn't I? After all, I am a rather cute bald woman!

When I first lost my hair a few months ago, I was picking up my daughter from school and I chatted with a dad through my car window. I apparently said...

When I first lost my hair a few months ago, I was picking up my daughter from school and I chatted with a dad through my car window. I apparently said something like: "I'm not very pretty right now."

As we drove away, my daughter said to me: "But you're beautiful."

And I realized that I had just done something I know we should never do with our daughters. By putting myself down, I was teaching her that it's okay to put herself down. Yikes!

FINDING BLESSINGS

It's funny how we often don't see how good we have it until we are blindsided with a daunting set of circumstances. During my first few chemo sessions, I didn't realize how lucky I was.

I had been warned about the hair, the nausea, the potential fatigue. But no one had prepared me for the murmurs and whispers in the corridor during my third chemo session.

"Yeah, we have a coronavirus case," a doctor said to someone in the hall.

The words pierced the air and set my heart racing. This was in the pre-pandemic era, when every whisper of Covid sent chills down our spines. At this point, the virus implied death, especially for someone with chemo-compromised immunity, where even a common cold could knock me down.

When Dr. Horkheimer came in, I shared my panic.

"One of your patients has Covid?"

He quickly clarified. "It's not one of our patients," he reassured, "but someone in town."

Oh, okay. Better. But still, this meant the disease was coming.

If the looming pandemic closed facilities, would my treatment halt midstream? The thought of starting all over again when I had already conquered a few sessions on this arduous journey was a weight I wasn't sure I could endure.

But Dr. Horkheimer, always the bearer of comforting news, assured me, "Even if we close, you'll continue your treatment elsewhere. You're not going to have an interruption in this schedule. That's simply not going to happen."

By the next session, though, not only would visitors be prohibited, but outside belongings as well. I wouldn't even be allowed to bring my blanket.

What a poignant reminder to cherish what we have, even when—*especially* when—our situations seem bleak.

It was chemotherapy. But I had the luxury of Rob's comforting presence by my side, a soft, fluffy blanket to warm my goosebumps as I chomped on ice.

I felt these blessings, but I took them for granted.

Covid reminded me that even in the midst of challenges, there are always silver linings, even the simple realization that things could always be tougher.

Adventure had taught me many things, but Gratitude kept showing me the light in the darkest tunnels.

Grab your Gratitude Amplifier Toolkit at
www.actuallyicanbook.com

TELL ME A JOKE

"Tell me a joke" is a common refrain in our household.

Rob will suddenly turn to Ellie and me with expectant eyes, waiting for a punchline. There's this unspoken challenge as we both sift through our mental archives, aiming to deliver a fresh dose of humor.

Sure, the pressure's on, and I sometimes fret over possibly letting him down. But it's heartwarming how humor weaves through our family tapestry, creating many bonds of shared chuckles.

As the days of chemotherapy piled up and lockdown began, I found myself wanting to be on the receiving end, hungry for a good laugh.

It wasn't just about jokes. I needed pockets of joy, momentary distractions from the heaviness. In this quest, I learned to unearth humor from the most unlikely places. The tougher the circumstance, the more determined I became to find its funny side.

A heartfelt, knee-slapping guffaw, especially one experienced amid traumatic or high-stress situations, is not only a nice distraction, but a medically prescribed act.

On the Monday night before my fourth round of the Red Devil regimen, I lay on my comfy beanbag chair in the family room while Hubby sat on the couch doing work on his computer. I suddenly felt my body tense up in fear.

"I don't want to go tomorrow," I said.

"I know," Rob said back to me. "I'm sorry."

The side effects from the last session were finally easing after almost two weeks, but they were going to start all over again with tomorrow's injections. I was panicking.

I felt like I was having PTSD, but it wasn't *post* anything.

"Maybe it's good I'm having PTSD now. I'm having DTSD (During Traumatic Stress Disorder). Then when it's all over, I'll have already dealt with that and I can move on."

To make circumstances even more frightful, an entire family in our area had come down with Covid, and several of them passed. Life was scary. Protocols were changing.

The next day, Rob drove me to the chemotherapy center as usual, but instead of coming in with me, he stayed in the parking lot. Guests were no longer allowed inside.

I checked in and stood in a state of fear and indecision. Was it safe to sit in a chair that someone else had just sat in? Would touching something be dangerous? How often should I wash my hands?

I worried all by myself. This was the first time I had to go through a day of treatment alone. The early stages of the pandemic, combined with the turmoil of chemotherapy, were taking their toll on me.

They called me into the small nurses' room to run through the pre-treatment activities—check my vitals, access my port, and draw blood. I waited to be taken into the chemotherapy room.

Choosing an available chair in a new section, I waited for a nurse to come over to hang all the pre-meds in my station and begin to drip the first one into my port.

After each one depleted, a loud beep notified the nurses, and someone would come over to switch out a new bag and begin the next drug.

There were four pre-meds. Then the real fun began. The Red Devil made his appearance!

At this point, just looking at that neon red liquid made me sick. But it was hard to not look.

During the pre-med drips, I could close my eyes or scroll on my phone and ignore what was actually going on. But because a nurse was sitting next to me delivering the Red Devil (and usually chatting with me to be friendly), and because I had to chew on ice nonstop for fifteen minutes, I couldn't easily escape reality with my usual tactics.

I had to get through this part by experiencing it fully.

Yuck.

Also, on this particular day, I had no one with me to distract me. But since I knew what was coming, I was prepared with a Facebook post.

Tell me a joke.

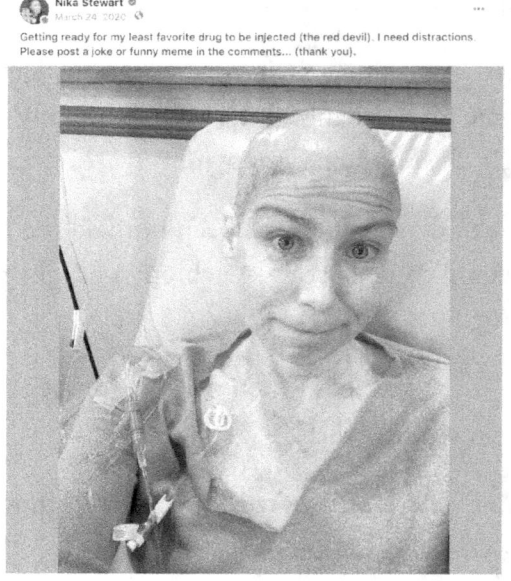

Getting ready for my least favorite drug to be injected (the red devil). I need distractions. Please post a joke or funny meme in the comments... (thank you).

As soon as I hit "post," comments began flooding in, turning my feed into a flurry of laughter and light-heartedness. Every new joke notification became a counterweight to the gravity of the red liquid entering my port.

When the Red Devil portion of my treatment was finished, I logged back on to see more than 100 funny memes, jokes, and stories.

Here are a few for your amusement.

I'd like to cancel my
3 month trial of 2020.
Not impressed.
Do not recommend.

(We were only a few weeks into the Pandemic. We had no idea what was coming!)

A curious mom uses her iPhone to text her daughter to ask a very important question. The text reads: "What does IDK, ILY, TTYL mean?" Before long the daughter texts back: I don't know, I Love You, Talk to you later. To which the mom responds,, "It's ok, don't worry about it, I'll ask your brother. Love you too!"

A five-dollar bill went into a bar and the bartender refused to serve him. The bartender said, "Sir, I'm sorry, but this is a singles bar."

You may be groaning now, but just imagine how much these corny little jokes did to lighten my mood! Not only was it a healthy and happy distraction from my treatment, but it also showed me how much my friends (and even strangers following my story) wanted to support me in my time of need.

I am truly blessed.

Add laughter to your day with your Find the Funny journal.
Download it at www.actuallyicanbook.com

THE ANTIDOTE TO ADVERSITY

Turning to social media wasn't just about documenting my journey, it was also my sanctuary. A place where I could redirect my energy, paint my narrative, express my inner thoughts and feelings, and find pockets of light in what often felt like never-ending darkness. For every daunting moment that tried to pull me down, there was a video idea or a song lyric that propped me right back up.

I was determined to dance through chemo. After a few very sickening weeks, I finally felt like I could see the light at the end of the tunnel. As dim as it was, I was pretty sure it was there.

Finally, I was able to have fun with a countdown. After each session, I creatively marked one less session on the whiteboard and recorded myself dancing, jumping, doing "flips," and being silly.

Each erasure of a chemo treatment on the whiteboard was a small victory, a step closer to the end. But what made the weekly countdown videos even more exciting was that I kept challenging myself to get more and more inventive. I was truly diving into my new hobby of creating videos.

Getting ready to hit the record button for my "Six to Go!" video, Rob, out of the blue, suggested, "Why not erase number seven, and then do a backflip?"

I raised my eyebrows, knowing he was pulling my leg. "Right, because I'm quite the gymnast," I retorted, sarcasm dripping from every word.

But Rob wasn't fazed. "Not an actual backflip," he clarified. "Just make it look like you did one."

I shot him a skeptical look. "I have no clue how to pull that off."

He just smirked. "You'll figure it out."

And with that, he sauntered off, leaving me clueless.

But curious.

Suddenly, I had an idea. What if I found a stock video of someone doing a backflip and superimposed it on a video of me? I thought that could possibly work.

I set up my phone and prepared the shot. After about a dozen attempts to jump in the air as if I was about to do a flip, and then several more pretending to land, I thought I had the right take.

I created the video. It was not high level. But it sure was fun.

I was documenting slices of my life—unpolished, spontaneous, and real. Yet, every time I hit the record button, an innate desire to elevate my content arose, not for perfection, but for the sheer joy of exploration. With each creation, I dove a little deeper into the art of video-making, teaching myself subtle nuances that would make the end product pop a bit more.

It wasn't about professional-grade videos, but about growth and evolution. It felt thrilling to learn a new editing trick, layer in a quirky sound effect, or time a transition just right. Every tweak was a step forward, ensuring that the videos not only documented my journey but also reflected my ever-growing palette of skills.

These forays into the digital world weren't just therapeutic, they were transformative. With every upload, I was not just sharing a piece of myself, but also showcasing my commitment to growth, innovation, and relentless curiosity.

I began to write song parodies, sharing the hilarity of having to choose from dozens of wigs, the insanity of being in lockdown for so long, and the oddities of being on Zoom all day.

And then came TikTok, the rising giant of the social media world. What better place to merge my love for music, video, and humor? The platform seemed designed for my brand of creativity. Every video posed a new challenge, a new story, and a new memory captured in a digital bottle. Through every post and parody, I wasn't just reaching out to others but also finding fragments of my old self and celebrating the emerging new one.

One morning as I pulled on a t-shirt, I instinctively reached up to pull my long hair out of the back of the neck hole. But there was no hair to sweep.

Later that evening, I went to the sink to wash up and brush my teeth. As always, I opened my drawer and took out a clip to hold my hair away from my face. But I had no hair to clip back.

When I bent over to pick up something off the floor, I instinctively went to tuck phantom strands behind my ears.

Moments of muscle memory kept me reaching up, trying to push back or adjust hair that wasn't there.

In another life, these habitual gestures might have caused pangs of sadness, reminding me of my loss. Yet, the sheer silliness of it all was undeniably comical.

An idea bubbled up inside me. What if I turned this absent-minded hair-flipping habit into a lighthearted video sketch for everyone? While the whole "forgetting-you're-bald" theme might not resonate universally, it had the potential to be a quirky, amusing watch.

I had a blast scripting and filming these subconscious antics. Three particularly amusing instances made the cut, complete with playful text animations and a catchy tune. Satisfied, I uploaded it to TikTok and called it a night.

Waking up the next day, my notifications were swamped. I had gained a whopping 3,000 new followers overnight!

A TIKTOK OBSESSION IS BORN

Gaining a surge of new followers gave me an adrenaline rush. The numbers kept ticking upward, and notifications continued to flood in. This was every content creator's dream! Yet, more than just excitement, it served as a profound revelation.

Here I was, thinking that my hairless quirks were unique oddities, totally unrelatable to the average person. But as the flood of comments on my video poured in, a realization dawned on me. The essence of my experience was universally human. It wasn't about being bald or having hair; it was about the comical blunders our brains lead us into, thanks to the routines we've unknowingly built over time.

One user commented, "Haha, this is so me when I push up my glasses that are already sitting right on my nose!"

Another said, "I've spent minutes searching for my phone while talking on it. Too relatable!"

It wasn't about hair or the lack thereof. It was about those amusing lapses we all have, reminding us of our habits, silly mistakes, and the funny ways our brains operate.

In this surprising way, my bald head became a bridge, connecting me to countless others, sharing chuckles over our idiosyncrasies.

One of the beautiful aspects of social media is how it can magnify shared experiences, turning a personal, intimate moment into a collective laugh. And as it turned out, this video wasn't just about showcasing my own life's peculiarities, but also about uncovering the delightful universal oddities that unite us all.

After posting this video on TikTok, I created "Part 2" and also posted it on YouTube, Instagram, and Facebook. The views kept accumulating. At one point, when the video topped the one-million-view mark, I could not keep up with the notifications. One million turned to two, three, and then ten million!

But it didn't stop there. As the weeks and months rolled on, so did the attention that video received. When it eclipsed ten million views, I felt I'd hit on an important theme—it was okay to laugh at ourselves.

More than two years later, this video continues to generate views and comments. As of this writing, more than 160 million people have viewed this video! And when tabulating the views of all my videos throughout my cancer journey, the number surpassed a quarter of a billion.

Creating videos, revealing my story, and sharing my unorthodox philosophy to overcoming adversity has served as a much-needed vehicle to get me through my ordeal, while inspiring millions of people along the way.

LOCK DOWN THAT ATTITUDE

Lockdown's grip on the world felt more oppressive each day, weighing heavier on our spirits. Social media feeds, news outlets, and personal conversations (on Zoom and overheard in the hospital halls) echoed the same melancholy tone.

In an age of isolation, we were all paradoxically sharing the same experience.

Except for me.

At least, that's what it felt like. I was already on a lockdown of sorts, having to keep my distance from people during my treatments to ensure I remained healthy.

Perhaps because I was grappling with my personal challenge, I was insulated, making it hard for me to relate to what the world was feeling. I couldn't quite pinpoint why I felt so disconnected, but I recognized that my perspective and attitude might be just the tools to lift others.

As the world seemed to spiral, a quiet call within nudged me forward. I felt an obligation to sprinkle some joy amidst the gloom.

One day, as the side effects of my most recent treatment were starting to clear, I posted a thought.

Nika Stewart
April 3, 2020 · 🌐

ATTITUDE is everything. If you want to feel better - even in really tough times, you need to develop a great attitude.

One suggestion: find the magic in every tough situation. This takes practice. Practice now. The more often you do this, the more instinctual it will become. I promise.

Be silly. Think ridiculous, optimistic thoughts. Be a Pollyanna. Develop your great attitude muscle memory!

Sending love and light to all of you, my friends. 😊

ATTITUDE is everything. If you want to feel better - even in really tough times, you need to develop a great attitude.

One suggestion: find the magic in every tough situation. This takes practice. Practice now. The more often you do this, the more instinctual it will become. I promise.

Be silly. Think ridiculous, optimistic thoughts. Be a Pollyanna. Develop your great attitude muscle memory!

Sending love and light to all of you, my friends. 😊

I wanted everyone to know that even in this tumultuous time, the power to uplift ourselves lies in our own hands. It wasn't about denying the pain or sidestepping the difficulties, but choosing to face them with a more optimistic perspective. To choose to dance in the rain.

Our reactions to life's harshest circumstances determine the course of our journey.

Our collective spirits may have been dampened by the lockdown, but we weren't alone. And since we couldn't change the circumstances, we could change our words, choose new emotions, and find the magic.

There is always magic. It just may be hiding . . . really well.

Being Pollyannaish wasn't about denying the truth; it was about recognizing the roses amidst the thorns.

Because I witnessed so much pain around me, and because I still needed outlets to distract me from my own discomfort, I made it my mission to add happiness during those trying times—not to ignore or trivialize the real hardships people were facing, but to add a splash of pleasure wherever I could.

Every post, every video, every comment became a pebble in the pond, creating ripples of positivity.

The world needed light, and I thought if I could be even the smallest flicker of a candle in someone's dark room, my mission would be accomplished.

Then I realized that *preaching* positivity was not as effective as simply *living* it.

TURN WHINE INTO SHINE

During the height of my illness, when my videos chronicled the most trying moments, a viewer posed a poignant question.

"Why is it that when you share about your pain, you're showered with love, and when I do the same, I encounter negativity?"

That perception sent me on an introspective journey to discern if perhaps I had been doing something distinctively different. And, sure enough, what stood out emerged crystal clear.

When you relay your experiences in an empowering, honest fashion—instead of resorting to social media for venting or sympathy-seeking—the reactions you receive tend to be steeped in understanding and admiration.

Often, individuals don't realize how their words might translate as mere complaints. In their eyes, they're simply narrating their genuine pain. However, there's an art to framing our narratives, a way to communicate that invites empathy, support, and connection, instead of deflecting it.

EXAMPLES OF TURNING A WHINY POST INTO A SHINY ONE	
WHINE	**SHINE**
My worst fears just came true. Went to the doctor to find out about my treatment plan and found out I have to have chemo AND radiation AND hormone inhibitors. I can't even begin to imagine what the side effects are going to be like. My life is a disaster!	I've always preached that you don't have to be an "either / or" person. In many situations, why not choose both? 😄 So it seems very fitting that when I got my reports that would tell me if I needed further treatment (radiation OR chemo OR hormone inhibitors), the answer would be… ALL. Soon I'll start my bountiful journey.
Just letting you know that I may be off social media for quite a while. I'm starting chemotherapy tomorrow and I'll probably lose my hair the week after. Prayers appreciated.	Good news. I get to go wig shopping! I've always wanted to try out different styles (and colors!) without the long-term commitment, and this is my chance! I'm really looking forward to going a little wild and crazy.
With all the pain we have to go through in the hospital, you'd think they would give you a comfortable robe to wear. After surgery, I can't reach my arm around to the back, so I can't stand up or my entire naked backside will show. Will this discomfort ever end?	My favorite part of being in the hospital is the highly fashionable robes. They even open in the back so your butt can enjoy some freedom.

RELEASE THE PERFECT IMAGE

It's a well-worn philosophy among business coaches that you should share your stories of hardship only once your ordeal is over, when you've gleaned important lessons and emerged transformed on the other side.

Many believe that we appear more resilient if we wait to unveil our challenges until after we've conquered them. Esteemed marketing gurus advocate for this, suggesting that raw vulnerabilities should be kept under wraps, and that only once they've scarred over should they be put on display.

This is often recommended as a way not only to uplift those who hear our stories, but to maintain our status as successful leaders.

But this perspective neglects the profound connections made during the messy times of a crisis. By sharing in real-time, we invite others into the heart of our journey, the very place where pain meets perseverance. This transparency can shatter barriers, inspire empathy, and foster a deeper sense of community.

Consider, for instance, the mother battling postpartum depression. While societal pressures might push her to showcase only the joyous moments with her newborn on social media, there may be a better way to authentically share what she is experiencing. By admitting her struggles—the sleepless nights not just because of a restless baby, but because of her own anxiety and sadness—she can help enlighten followers about the depression some women experience surrounding motherhood and provide support for countless others in a similar position.

Think of the young man freshly graduated from college and unable to find a job in his field. Rather than only sharing the highlight reel of interviews and job offers, he also chooses to share the rejection letters, the moments of doubt, and the side gigs he takes up to pay the bills. By doing so, he gives a voice to the unspoken challenges many graduates face, fostering a sense of camaraderie and mutual understanding.

And the individual recovering from a breakup, who, instead of just presenting a facade of strength, chronicles the healing process—the good days filled with newfound freedoms and the rough nights consumed by loneliness. Such honesty can serve as a beacon for others navigating the choppy waters of heartbreak, reminding them it's okay to grieve, to heal at their own pace, and to seek support when needed.

Each of these narratives, like mine, underscores a powerful principle: in a world that often teaches us to conceal our perceived weaknesses, to bury the parts of our stories that don't fit a polished narrative, there's transformative power in embracing and showcasing our full truths, even when the story is not pretty.

When we reveal those aspects we've been conditioned to feel shame around, we inadvertently grant others the permission to feel okay, to acknowledge that they are enough. We offer solace to those silently battling similar issues, reassuring them they are not alone. By sharing the things that others only wish they could voice, we create an environment where authenticity reigns supreme, and where the messy, complicated, yet beautiful mosaic of human experience is celebrated.

It's not just about being honest and authentic, it's about affirming the joys, sorrows, and complexities of being human.

I hope that my journey of unveiling my battles, particularly during the most trying phases, serves as an allegory for all women who've felt pressured to mask their challenges.

We're told to hide our missteps, to cloak our imperfections until they can be presented as neatly packaged lessons. But there's power in the raw, unfiltered truth. There's strength in solidarity. And by sharing our stories, even mid-struggle, we not only help ourselves, but also potentially light the way for others navigating the same storms.

CAN'T HOLD THIS BEACH BALL DOWN

As the world closed its doors and windows, and we all retreated to the safe confines of our homes, a wave of creativity surged as people devised innovative solutions to maintain human connection. Online hangouts became the new Friday nights. People sought ways to interact, to be together while apart, to find silver linings in a clouded reality.

One evening, a friend texted me an invitation to a virtual beach party on Zoom. While many attendees simply threw on a beach-themed background or donned their favorite swimsuit, I saw an opportunity for a unique twist. I transformed my bald head into a vibrant beach ball, using colorful lip paints.

Tonight I attended a virtual dinner party.
The theme was SUMMER. So I brought a beach ball.
(Courtesy of a few colorful lip pallets)

I felt so grateful and lucky to have this blank canvas to paint on.

Joining the party, my new "beach ball" was an instant hit. While most were amazed at the artwork, the conversations invariably veered toward my ongoing battle with cancer. And a sentiment I heard repeatedly was, "Wow, it must be so tough for you, dealing with this during such a challenging time."

But here's the twist in my tale.

I actually found the lockdown to be a sort of blessing in disguise. While the world fretted about being indoors, it provided me an unexpected reprieve, a diversion from the weight of my medical battles. Instead of the dual pressures of navigating both the outside world and my health, I only had to focus on one.

We all have the ability to choose our focus, decide how we respond to situations, and find unique and creative outlets, even in the toughest of times. For me, the lockdown became an avenue to divert my attention from the medical charts and appointments to the canvas of my head and the warm virtual company of friends and family.

My beach ball wasn't just about painting my head. It was a testament to the power of choice.

In that decision to get creative and playful, I found joy and strength, reminding not just me but everyone around that no matter the circumstances, we can always find a way to cha-cha through a challenge, dance in the downpour, sway in the storm.

TRANSITIONING TO TAXOL: SILVER LININGS IN EVERY SYRINGE

The day had come for a pivotal shift in my treatment. Good-bye, Red Devil, and hello, Taxol!

I couldn't help but greet this change with a blend of anticipation and optimism. The notorious side effects of the Red Devil had been a relentless companion for what felt like an eternity. The prospect of those symptoms fading into the background was incredibly appealing.

Yet, as with all transitions, there's an element of the unknown. Taxol was new terrain, an unfamiliar concoction that my body had yet to encounter. This "new poison," as I fondly referred to it, was a wild card.

As I sat in that chemo center, awaiting the new drug infusion, apprehension gripped me. The medical staff told me that due to my body's unfamiliarity with the drug, the first Taxol treatment would be slow and deliberate, spanning several hours. They were prepped to combat any negative reaction, but the thought of being in that chair for four to five hours seemed daunting.

And actually, appealing.

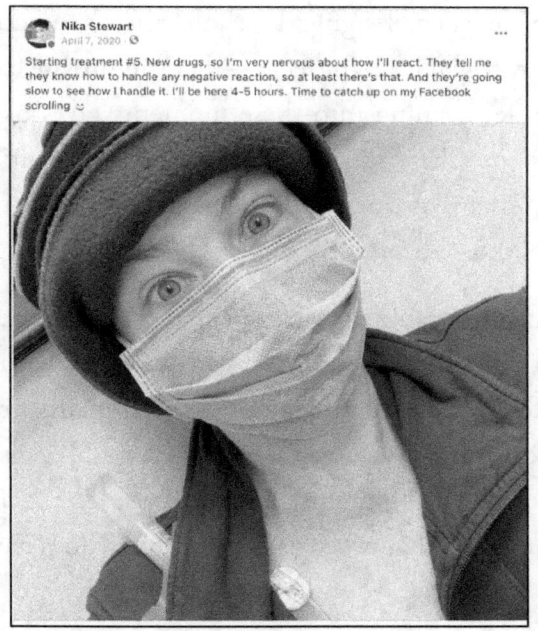

Starting treatment #5. New drugs, so I'm very nervous about how I'll react. They tell me they know how to handle any negative reaction, so at least there's that. And they're going slow to see how I handle it. I'll be here 4-5 hours. Time to catch up on my Facebook scrolling. 😄

In this situation, there was a hidden gem—a sliver of positivity waiting to be acknowledged. I remember chuckling to myself and posting online about my unexpected, extended opportunity to catch up on my Facebook scrolling.

It sounds small, I know, but at that moment, I took it as my glimmer of positivity.

The magic lies in shifting our focus. It's about recognizing that even in the most challenging situations, there's something—no matter how trivial it might seem—that can provide comfort or even a smile. Leaning into these moments gives us strength. By tuning into these nuances of positivity, we equip ourselves with a mindset that can make seemingly insurmountable challenges a bit more bearable.

There's an undeniable power in positivity, and sometimes, all it takes is a tiny glimmer of hope or humor. Whether it's enjoying a few hours of uninterrupted social media browsing, a kind word from a nurse, or the warmth of a blanket in a cold room, these small moments can be our beacon. They fortify us, reminding us that every dark cloud truly does have a silver lining.

The trick? Never stop looking for it.

~~~

By the middle of April, with days growing longer, the weather in the Northeast US typically becomes warmer. But on this particular day, the house seemed unusually dark and chilly.

The cold cast a shadow over my mood as I thought of the next day's impending Taxol treatment #2.

Since the medical team saw that I could handle the new drug, the full treatment would go quicker. The full protocol would last about two and a half hours.

The pre-medications were easy. One drug that I received before the chemo was actually sweet! It was an antihistamine that made my body feel relaxed. So relaxed that I could close my eyes and sleep right through the one-hour chemo drip.

Except . . .

Instead of chomping on ice chips like I did during the Red Devil treatment, Taxol demanded another kind of endurance. I had to protect my fingers and toes from neuropathy by immersing my hands and feet in ice for the entire hour the drug dripped into my veins.

I found that uncomfortable, to say the least. The treatment room was kept cool, and even without the ice bath, I felt the need to bundle up in blankets.

The cold of my house that day made the anticipation of that icy ordeal even more dreadful.

Yet, standing in front of the mirror, my lack of hair brought a new perspective. The empty canvas of my scalp called to me. My gaze drifted to the row of wigs, each with its own character and flair. As I chose one and slipped it on, I felt not only physically warmer, but I also felt the warmth of empowerment and the thrill of choice.

It's chilly in the house today. Most people would put on a jacket. I threw on some hair.

#allwiggedupandnowheretogo

ALONG FOR THE RIDE

As I continued to post my chemo countdown videos online, the digital tally of my treatments began to feel less like individual posts and more like a collective journey. Every update drew my community closer to my experience. It felt like they were actually on the ride with me, eagerly counting down each treatment.

And their comments weren't just words. They were virtual hugs, pep talks, and shared anticipation.

Here's some of what they had to say:

So much fun getting to be more and more into your life. 😊 *you are really fun*

Wish I could come and help you erase...we will celebrate for sure...

Yay! Thank you for your inspiration.

Yes!!!! One erase at a time... awesome.

Let's schedule a virtual party to ring the bell with you!

I am in awe of your courage and strength. Your determination and positive outlook is an inspiration to everyone you touched with your daily updates.

I'm so happy for you. The end of this thing is in sight.

Woo Hoo. I am dancing too!!! Celebrating your finish line.

Cheering you on to that finish line with prayers for strength and humor, and ultimately, health!

I love you. And when this chemo is over I will do a dance for you my darling

Dance party!!!

Dancing with you my sister! You got me up off my butt!

Opening up about my journey became a therapeutic outlet, but it also seemed to resonate deeply with others. And the feedback loop of encouragement was powerful. My friends—new and old—felt my highs and lows as their own.

The beauty of this shared experience was that, by letting them in, we all became intertwined in a web of support. It wasn't just about my battle with cancer anymore—it was about the universal human experience of facing adversity, finding hope, and drawing strength from each other.

I began to feel that my story was not just for me anymore. It became a light for many who were navigating their own challenges.

Sharing was indeed healing, for me and for an entire community that came together in solidarity.

Get support on sharing your own story in an authentic and powerful way at www.actuallyicanbook.com

Hit Me, Baby

As I was browsing TikTok one day, the familiar strains of Britney Spears' "Hit Me Baby One More Time" caught my ear. But this particular version had a twist—an intensity, a potent rhythm with strong beats that seemed to capture my mood.

That iconic line, "Hit me baby one more time," resonated deeply, symbolizing the penultimate step before my final treatment. A rush of excitement washed over me.

I immediately bookmarked the track, my mind whirring with ideas. Even though my concluding treatment was still months away, this song had instilled a newfound anticipation, not just for the end of the treatments, but for the epic video I envisioned.

The thought of creating something that would evoke powerful emotions, perhaps even send shivers down spines, felt invigorating. This video would not only be about marking the end but also celebrating the spirit of endurance and fun, and I couldn't wait to bring it to life.

As I pressed on with my treatments, the anticipation of creating this video became a motivating force, pushing me through some challenging moments.

As you read further, keep that sense of eager anticipation alive. Later in these pages, I'll unveil the story with screenshots of this video masterpiece that encapsulates so much more than just the end of chemo.

The grand reveal awaits, and trust me, it is worth the anticipation!

PANDEMIC PARODIES

As I continued my weekly chemo infusions, the one-hour round-trip drive, once bustling with traffic, became eerily silent. The pandemic had the world in its grip, and suddenly, our collective reality had changed. As doors closed and masks went on, a mutual anxiety about basic necessities, from food to toilet paper, surged.

The global weight pressed down on all of us. News stories filled with cautionary tales blended with a scary sense of the unknown. Every conversation was about the virus, the scarcity of supplies, and the overwhelming uncertainty.

Never had there been such a collective relatability, as we all navigated the shared challenges and fears of a world in lockdown.

While many lamented the confinement, I found solace in my newfound love: relatable music parodies.

I found myself noticing the little quirks of this new "normal."

Why was my daughter spending so many hours on TikTok?

How was it possible that my mother still couldn't understand how to log onto Zoom?

And should we discuss the unspoken rule of virtual meetings? Business on top, pajamas (or nothing) down below.

These snippets of pandemic life became the inspiration for my music parodies. Encouraged by the influx of comments on my initial videos, I felt a drive to create entertaining segments that would resonate universally, giving us all a shared moment of levity amidst the chaos.

I wrote lyrics, and my laptop transformed into a makeshift recording studio.

Creating these parodies became therapeutic, a way to deal with the grim reality while highlighting the shared, sometimes humorous, experiences of lockdown life. The themes were relatable, from the endless allure of pizza (and the subsequent weight gain) to the adventures of teaching technology to parents.

Pizza Pie

The heartbreaking story of a loving, but toxic, relationship gone wrong. 🙂 🎶

"Though it will go to my rear end,
I can't abandon my best friend."

Who is YOUR best friend in quarantine?

Ever try to teach your mom tech? 🧑

(I added some curls to my wig and put on false eyelashes. I think I almost look like my old self!)

Teaching Zoom to My Mom

Ever try to teach your mom tech? 🧑

*(I added some curls to my wig and put on false eyelashes.
I think I almost look like my old self!)*

Enjoy these videos at www.actuallyicanbook.com

What started as a solo venture soon grew into a communal effort. Friends shared suggestions of songs to use and even wrote lyrics for me to record. I reached out to my community, urging them to send in their own video clips to be integrated into my musical productions. The response delighted me.

My flooded inbox included delicious snippets of people dancing in their living rooms, singing along, or acting out scenes from their quarantine routines. My parodies had transformed into collective anthems of resilience, humor, and relatable experiences.

Every video premiere became a virtual event, a brief escape from the gloom. Friends, family, and strangers tuned in, commenting, laughing, and amplifying the joy. These parodies formed timestamps of a world grappling with change, finding light amid the shadows.

As I navigated the dual challenges of chemotherapy and a world in lockdown, my parodies became another lifeline, another testament to the human spirit's ability to find humor, connection, and creativity, even in the bleakest of times.

As each song ended, and the applause rang out in virtual comments and emoji-filled reactions, it reminded me that no matter how dark the days, there's always a song waiting to be sung.

So I continued to sing.

FIND THE FUNNY SIDEBARS?

Whose hair dis?

I just found a long, dark hair on my shirt

Don't Do It, Girl!

Jumping in on a popular TikTok sound, where people were revealing something surprising, like a haircut or unexpected hair color, I walked on screen carrying a hair clipper box.

Voiceover: Girl, don't do it. It's not worth it.

Me: I'm not gonna do it, Girl. I was just thinking about it.
I'm not gonna do it.

(Walks off camera for a moment, then walks back in)

Me: I did it.

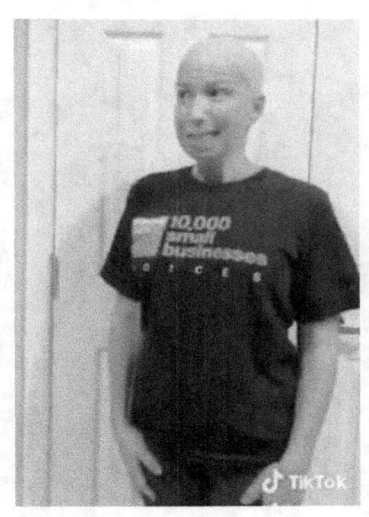

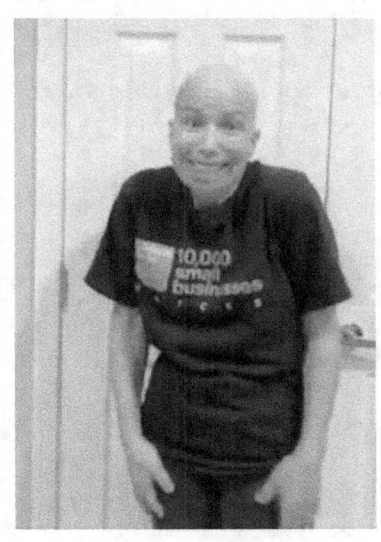

Spot the Difference

Nika Stewart
July 25, 2020 · 🌐

···

These "Spot the Difference" games are getting harder.

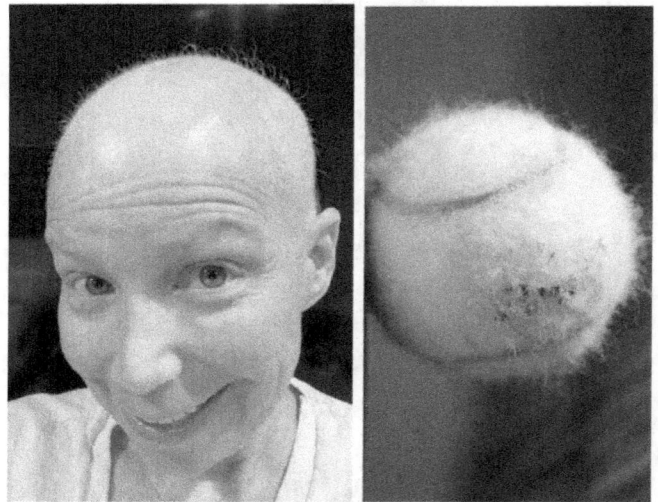

These "Spot the Difference" games are getting harder.

PINTS OF POSITIVITY: SAVORING SMALL JOYS

The simple beauty of life's smaller moments often, strangely, counterbalanced the immense challenges of embracing cancer. Those moments, especially when they caught me off guard, had an unexpected power to refocus my perspective.

One afternoon, when the chemo side effects were extraordinarily strong, the doorbell rang.

Rob yelled from his office that he was in the middle of a call, so with effort, I pushed myself up off my comfy beanbag chair and made my way to the door.

There on my porch sat a nondescript cardboard box. The sender's name wasn't immediately apparent. I took the box into my family room and curiously opened it, half-expecting some piece of medical equipment.

But as I peeled back the flaps, a waft of cold air greeted me. Nestled within a lining of dry ice were six beautiful pints of Java chip ice cream.

A smile broke across my face, and delight filled my entire body. This particular flavor had been my unique sanctuary in the early days of chemotherapy. While most foods were losing their flavor or becoming unappetizing, Java chip ice cream had miraculously retained its zest, bringing joy during those nauseating days.

Apparently, I had mentioned this in a video, and my friend Catherine, miles away, remembered. She had tucked away my offhand remark and, recognizing the significance of such a detail, acted on it.

In that moment, while cradling a pint of Java chip ice cream, happiness flooded my spirit. It wasn't just ice cream; I savored the sweetness of life and the deep connections that came from shared experiences.

It's often the smallest brushstrokes that make the painting beautiful.

A simple act—or a pint of ice cream—can turn around a day. In fact, it can even change your entire narrative.

The Challenge of Positivity

Pointing out the unfavorable aspects of our circumstances requires little effort. These easy complaints might even elicit sympathy.

But focusing on the joy in everyday moments? Now, that's a lot more challenging.

Turns out, it's in our nature to latch onto the negative. We remember pain more vividly than pleasure. Psychologists refer to this as the "negativity bias." Our brains are naturally inclined to give more attention to negative experiences over neutral or positive ones.

But what if, instead of succumbing to this bias, we consciously choose joy? The day that Java chip ice cream arrived at my door is proof of the transformative power of unexpected delights. I could have continued to lament about my chemo side-effects or how I missed the taste of my favorite foods. The ice cream, however, brought joy and a reminder that life's pleasures often come in small, unexpected packages.

Research has repeatedly demonstrated the benefits of maintaining a positive outlook. A study published in the *Journal of Personality and Social Psychology* found that expressing gratitude, even in the face of challenges, can lead to increased well-being and reduced depression.

It's not just about feeling good momentarily. The act of focusing on the positive can rewire our brains over time. In fact, by practicing gratitude, we strengthen neural pathways that make it easier and more natural to focus on the positive.

Another study from *Harvard Medical School* suggests that gratitude can improve overall heart health, especially for those at risk of cardiac diseases. Grateful people tend to lead healthier lives. They exercise more, eat better, and take better care of their health, leading to beneficial outcomes like improved sleep and resilience to stress.

One Step Further

In our pursuit of gratitude, we often think of the obvious blessings—the support of friends and family, the beauty of a sunset, the joy of an unexpected treat. But true growth in gratitude pushes us to venture beyond the conventional, to find gratitude in the seemingly negative experiences of our lives.

Being grateful for something like cancer might sound absurd, if not downright masochistic, to many. How can one be thankful for pain, for the countless hours spent in chemo, or for days confined to a bed while healing? But herein lies the transformative power of a counterintuitive approach to gratitude.

Each experience, no matter how harsh, teaches us something. Cancer taught me about my strength, resilience, and the depths of love and support from those around me. The grueling hours in chemo, while physically and emotionally draining, became moments of introspection and reevaluating what truly matters in life. Lying in bed wasn't just a recovery; it was a chance to pause, reflect, and deeply connect with my own thoughts and emotions.

Now let me clarify. Being grateful for these experiences doesn't mean I'd willingly choose them or wish them on anyone. Instead, it's about recognizing the unique silver linings that come with them, and the insights and growth they bring.

Research shows that people who have faced significant adversities in life, such as serious illnesses or major accidents, and have learned to find meaning and benefits from such experiences, tend to exhibit higher levels of life satisfaction compared to those who have faced fewer adversities or hadn't discerned any positive aspects from their challenges.

This isn't just about adopting a "glass half full" perspective, but truly about discovering transformative growth from within the most daunting circumstances.

Being grateful for life's challenges pushes us to dive deep, way beyond the surface level of everyday thankfulness. It urges us to look at life holistically, valuing every twist and turn for the lessons and insights they bring.

By acknowledging and being thankful for the trials of life, we free ourselves from the bitterness that can often accompany hardship. Instead of becoming embroiled in "why me?" sentiments, we empower ourselves to ask, "What can I learn? How can I grow? What unexpected silver linings can I focus on?"

Dive deep into gratitude with our Gratitude Amplifier Toolkit at www.actuallyicanbook.com

ONE TO GO:
THE COUNTDOWN BALLET

The time had at last arrived to record my penultimate chemo countdown video! I had been producing it in my head for months, working out all the subtle nuances to make this a memorable piece.

Looking back on my journey through social media, I have to say this video is my favorite because it brings back the sense of excitement and achievement I felt after completing so many chemo treatments.

Here's the setup and script:

Setting: The corner of a hall at the bottom of a staircase, sunlight filtering in from a side door casting the area in a

*soft light. Center screen is the whiteboard, leaning against the wall, its bold lettering—**CHEMO TO GO**—in stark contrast with the sixteen thin lines below it. The board seems to hum with a silent gravity.*

The protagonist stands in front of the board, allowing the weight of those sixteen lines to sink in, a visible reminder of her long journey, each line representing another monumental event.

On cue, a familiar song plays, the powerful beats echoing through the room.

Close-up on her face, a myriad of emotions plays out: determination, anticipation, courage. The beats dictate her movement as she meets the gaze of the audience from different angles. Each look conveys a story—a story that had been told, and another that was to come.

With every lyric she lip-syncs, her connection to the song becomes evident. "My loneliness is killing me," she mouths, the raw vulnerability in her eyes contrasting with the strength of her stance.

The scene heightens as she begins her dance with the whiteboard.

With every beat, a line disappears. It's a playful tango, a dance of triumph. She blows on the board, and one line vanishes. Snap! Another fades. The traditional eraser comes into play, and a few more lines are gone. It's choreographed chaos, every movement filled with meaning.

Hope grows with the song's crescendo. Seven beats, seven more lines. Her hand moves with precision, each erasure a symbol of another treatment past, another battle won. The weight in the hall seems to lift, replaced with an electrifying anticipation.

Then, the most potent moment . . .

Directly facing the audience, chest thumping in time with "Hit Me Baby," the raw emotion is palpable, a declaration to the world.

The final line on the board becomes her dance partner, circled with fervor, over and over to the words "One More Time."

As the last powerful beat of the song rings out, she turns and gives the camera a piercing look, capturing the essence of her triumph, defiance, and, most importantly, determination.

The video wasn't just for me (although it was such a joy planning, scripting, recording, and editing it). It was for every person who had followed my journey, every individual who had sent positive vibes, every new friend who felt they were on the ride with me, and everyone undergoing their own personal battles.

It was an homage to human resilience and to the power of community and support. With every line erased, I hoped they felt the excitement, the relief, and the profound message that there's power in numbers, strength in community, and joy in adversity.

Of course, this was not the end. But it was close to the end of the most difficult physical and emotional challenge I'd ever faced. And that tiny glow at the end of the tunnel—the one that I couldn't even believe was there a few months earlier—was growing brighter.

You can watch the One To Go video at
www.actuallyicanbook.com

NO BELL TO RING, BUT . . .

The final chemo session became a day of bittersweet contrasts.

The anticipation of reaching this milestone was palpable, but the somber atmosphere of the treatment center under pandemic restrictions and the sadness I felt that no one would be with me during this triumphant session cast a shadow on the event.

I tried not to focus on my biggest disappointment—not being able to celebrate with family and friends.

But I came prepared to bring a little brightness with me—a large platter for the medical team, brimming with vibrant cupcakes and adorned with fluttering flags and gleaming metallic streamers. These weren't just sweets, they were my offering of appreciation, a symbol of the journey coming to a close, and my way of thanking the tireless staff who had been with me every step of the way.

And a fun treat.

Sitting in the chemo chair, the rhythmic whirr and beep of machines accompanying my thoughts, I watched as staff members occasionally walked past the room. Their eyes, the only visible part of their expressions because of the Covid masks we were all wearing, widened with surprise as they spotted the colorful cupcakes. The atmosphere lightened as each squealed with joy when they learned the purpose of the pastries.

A particularly thoughtful nurse asked if she might distribute the cupcakes among the other patients. Warmth spread within me as I readily agreed.

I smiled as I watched my fellow patients pull down their masks and nibble on the treats.

As the nurse leaned toward one woman and offered her a cupcake, she curiously inquired about the occasion. The nurse pointed to me and explained that I brought them to celebrate my final session.

She looked across the room and congratulated me. I asked how many sessions she had left, excited to celebrate the countdown with her.

"Oh, I don't have an end. I need to have chemo for the rest of my life."

A rush of emotions enveloped me. The profound weight of her words juxtaposed with my journey momentarily stole my breath. Suddenly, my months of chemo, while challenging, felt so conveniently temporary compared to her indefinite timeline.

The day had started with feelings of disappointment, threaded with the joy of concluding my treatments. But this chance interaction offered a new perspective. The challenges I'd faced were undeniably tough, but others carried heavier burdens. I was reminded of the vast spectrum of experiences and the relative nature of our individual hardships.

I felt deeply fortunate, and my heart brimmed with gratitude. While my path had been strewn with apprehension and pain, it also had an end—that light at the end of the tunnel. And now, I wasn't just celebrating the end of my chemo, I was celebrating the gift of perspective, the appreciation of my journey, and the profound gratitude for the path I was walking.

And then, I got a text.

Glancing down, I saw Rob's name on the screen, likely marking his presence in the parking lot, awaiting my exit. But the preview showed a curious, yet familiar, face—the Soup Nazi from Seinfeld!

Rob, always finding ways to sprinkle humor into our journey, had probably crafted another one of his surprises. However, just as I was about to delve into his message, the nurses enthusiastically approached me, presenting a certificate accompanied by a bag of goodies.

Their gesture, brimming with warmth, momentarily took center stage. We rejoiced together, marking the conclusion of a journey they had accompanied me on.

The air was thick with sentiments of joy, pride, relief, and an underlying note of bittersweetness. As much as I yearned for this conclusion, there was an unexpected tug at my heartstrings. Endings, no matter how eagerly anticipated, always stir a sense of loss in me.

I would miss the camaraderie, the newfound friends, and even the routine that had become a part of my life.

Emerging from the chemo center, a delightfully warm summer day greeted me, a stark contrast to the cold treatment room where I had sat with my hands and feet in ice. Ah, summer. The perfect season to warm my body and spirit.

Rob's text remained unread. As I slid into the car, his excitement mirrored my anticipation. He had indeed sent me a video, and not just any video. It was the actor who had played the Soup Nazi, looking directly into the camera with that signature sternness.

In a familiar tone, he proclaimed, "Nika! No more chemo for you!"

Yes, Rob had hired Larry Thomas to record this for me!

Rob's unique sense of humor, combined with the novelty and thoughtfulness of the gesture, made this moment unforgettable. Though the chemo center lacked a ceremonial bell to ring—a common tradition in many centers—this customized video became my symbolic chime.

"Nika, no chemo for you! Come back…NEVER!"

I MAY HAVE LOST A LOT

The day after my final treatment, inspiration hit within me. I felt compelled to encapsulate my adventurous journey, not merely for myself, but for others who might embark on a similar path. What unfolded was a poignant, thirty-second visual memoir that wasn't just about the losses, but about the tenacity of spirit.

The video I produced began with a stark declaration: *First, I lost my breasts.*

An image of me in the hospital right after the mastectomy accompanied the text.

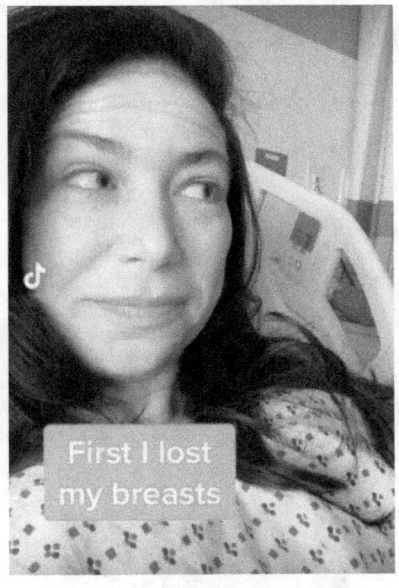

As the video went on, each statement cataloged another loss, another sacrifice to the unrelenting journey of cancer:

> *Then I lost my hair.*
> *I lost my strength.*
> *I lost my eyelashes.*
> *I lost my fitness and flexibility.*

There were clips of my once lustrous hair, morphing into a bald head, snapshots highlighting the ebbing away of my strength, and a moment capturing my unusual-looking lash-less eyes.

Yet, with each visual and each phrase, a narrative emerged, not one of unending sorrow, but of *resilience*.

Of course, there was the grueling, relentless stripping away of what was once familiar. But then the video pivoted to its uplifting and contrasting final message:

But I didn't lose my smile.

Despite the evident physical changes and challenges, there it was—my smile, unwavering and genuine.

That smile represented so much more than happiness. It was a symbol of my rebellion against following the common path, a manifestation of my spirit's refusal to be subdued.

In thirty seconds, this video spoke volumes about who I was, not just as a cancer patient, but as an individual. It is an ode to every person's ability to blaze our own trails, "right" our own stories, and create our own powerful, authentic lives.

While my journey was punctuated with numerous losses, this brief biographical video affirmed one crucial victory—the indomitable spirit of a woman who refused to let her circumstances steal her essence.

This video remains a pivotal artifact of my journey, echoing the spirit and attitude I carried and shared.

HIT THE ROAD, CHUCK

I had been told the side effects might linger, possibly for years, but with each day, I hoped for a tangible sign of improvement. That sign took its time arriving.

The chemotherapy portion of my treatment was over. But before I could breathe easy, my oncologist had other plans.

A reminder about a scan from the early days of my diagnosis resurfaced. A tiny node in the center of my chest had once been a concern. Back then, it was just a blip on a screen. It could have been an innocuous result of my surgeries or something more sinister. The thought had been if it were malignant, the chemo would take care of it. With everything else on my plate, I had shelved this concern at the back of my mind.

But now that node moved to the forefront. We needed a scan to see if the size had changed.

Three days post-chemo, I had the scan. And as fate would have it, the results, although ready in a day, kept us in suspense over a long weekend.

In the interim, I bid adieu to Chuck, my trusty port. For almost half a year, this device had been my ally, making the intrusions of chemo a tad more bearable. Its removal was a symbol of the end of one chapter with the promise of new beginnings.

When Monday finally graced us, the results brought relief. The node had shrunk. In fact, it was gone. Yet, my doctor didn't seem satisfied.

"The dilemma," he said, "is that we're not sure if it was a benign anomaly or a cancerous cell reduced by the chemo."

I struggled to see the issue. It had shrunk. Wasn't that cause for celebration?

But the doctor insisted on a cautious approach. The uncertainty around that node warranted a more aggressive radiation plan, taking every precaution to ensure that no malignancy returned.

Nevertheless, the overarching news was positive. The scan was clean, and my body was free from any evident dark spots. With this news, my spirits lifted, readying myself for the next leg of my journey: radiation.

SELF-MADE WOMAN

Arnold Schwarzenegger said something that resonated deeply with me. He stated that calling him a "self-made man" would be a misrepresentation. He believed that every individual who guided, supported, and lifted him played an integral role in his journey. That declaration of interconnectedness echoed sentiments I've felt throughout my voyage.

Facing the monumental challenge of cancer, I've had the opportunity to experience the profound truth behind Arnold's words. If anyone were to look at my journey and say, "Nika is so self-assured and brave," they would be missing the essence of my story. Yes, I faced my challenges head-on, with determination and optimism, but the strength to do so didn't solely come from within.

Each step of the way, I felt an invisible force of love and support wrapping around me like a warm blanket on those freezing chemo days. My family was my rock, their love guiding me through even when my optimism wavered. My friends, with their continuous check-ins, words of encouragement, and gestures of care, lit my darker moments.

And it wasn't just those close to me. A collective of amazing souls from social media, most of whom I'd never met in person, sent waves of love, encouragement, and positivity. Each message, comment, and share gave proof of the boundless empathy and connection humans are capable of.

These interactions, these bonds, and these gestures—big and small—have been the wind beneath my wings, lifting me higher and propelling me forward when my own strength faltered. They reminded me that while the battle was mine, I wasn't alone in the war. Every cheer infused me with resilience.

Like Arnold, I believe no one truly goes through life's battles alone. And in my heart, I know that the positivity with which I faced my challenge was deeply intertwined with the love and support that poured in from every corner of my world.

RADIATION READINESS

The transition from chemo to radiation was not a seamless one. It involved new preparations, a fresh understanding, and another set of frustrations to navigate.

But it was awesome!

In my mind, nothing in the world would be as bad as chemo. I had a fresh appreciation for things I used to take for granted. Compared to chemo, every new challenge felt easy.

My first step was a meeting with the radiation oncologist to determine the right course of action. She was lovely. And so young. Thankfully, she appeared competent and confident.

She explained that radiation therapy works by using high-energy rays to destroy cancer cells, targeting the specific regions where the cancer resides.

One of the first tasks at hand was to evaluate my breast expanders. They had to ensure the radiation beams would be unobstructed. It turned out the left expander would be in the way of one of the beam's paths.

That meant another appointment with Dr. Griffith. Remember how I had planned to have the expanders filled little by little until it was time for the reconstruction? Well, now we were removing some fluid so my body would be free from obstruction. My left expander had to be deflated so there would be an uninterrupted path.

I assumed we would be deflating both sides. But the surgeon's preference was to actually overfill the radiated side. This would aid in a more favorable reconstruction outcome later on.

The result? A lopsided appearance, one I had to come to terms with for the next couple of months.

For the precision that radiation therapy requires, my body became a canvas for the technical aspects of the treatment. To ensure consistent alignment for each of the thirty scheduled sessions, I received my very first tattoos! They were four tiny dots on my chest and side.

In addition, a custom breast mold was crafted, designed to protect the targeted area and ensure it remained immobile.

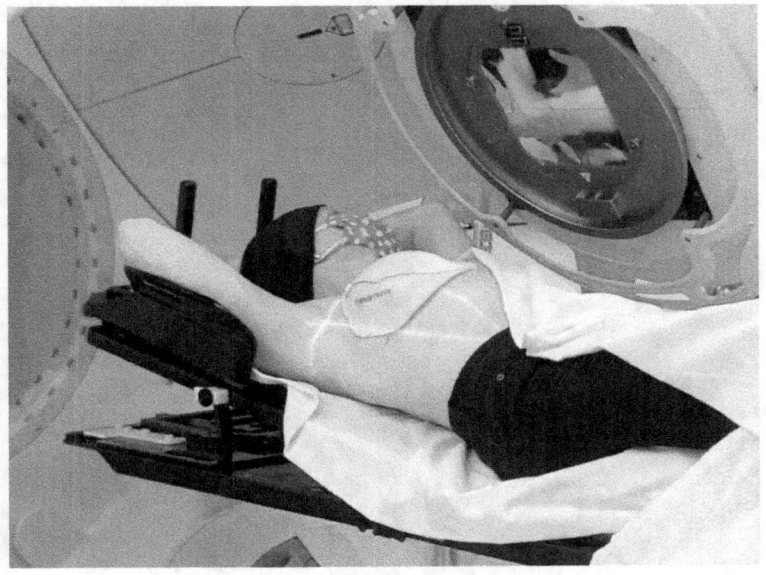

The nurse methodically explained the daily routine. Every day, I would check in, sanitize my hands (still the era of COVID-19), change into a robe, and await my turn. In the treatment room, I'd discard the robe, recline on the cool metal bed, wear my breast mold, and turn my head in preparation. As the technicians exited, I would be left alone with the machine. Guided by a series of beeps, I'd hold my breath when prompted. The procedure, short-lived at about seven minutes, became a routine I perfected over time.

Ironically, the travel time exceeded the treatment duration, making the thirty-minute drive seem silly. I often found myself wishing the session was a tad longer, allowing me more moments to unwind. But perhaps it was a blessing in disguise, as fatigue was one of the side effects I'd been warned about.

Opting for the last available slot ensured I could wrap up my day with the treatment and retreat home, seeking the comfort of my bed. This daily pilgrimage to the treatment center became my new, albeit temporary, normal.

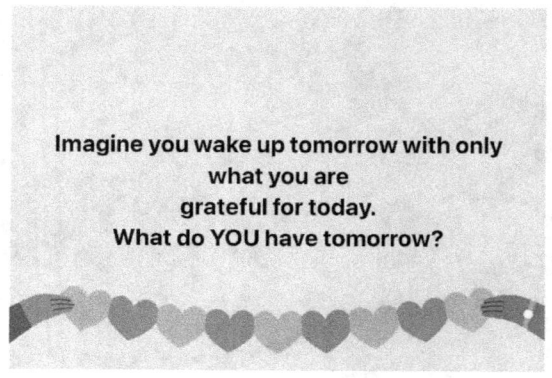

Imagine you wake up tomorrow with only
what you are
grateful for today.
What do YOU have tomorrow?

DANCING WITH LYMPHEDEMA

As I continued to journey through the maze of cancer treatments, each new challenge that emerged began to feel less like a setback and more like a call to strength. With every ache or unfamiliar procedure, renewed determination grew within me.

I tried to embrace these challenges with a mix of curiosity and resilience. Each obstacle, instead of dampening my spirits, fueled a deeper commitment to healing and well-being.

No, I was not perfect at this. And yes, an unexpected setback caused disappointment and fear at first.

As I was adjusting to the routine of radiation, this newfound mindset was once again put to the test. My right arm showed signs of swelling.

I tried to think of this as not just a physical symptom to address, but as a test of my resolve and adaptability.

Yet the possibility of lymphedema—an irreversible swelling caused by a blockage in the lymphatic system—loomed.

When the surgeon removed eighteen of my lymph nodes, she had cautioned about this very risk. With a compromised lymphatic system, my body would struggle to remove excess fluid in the arm. This fluid could build up from a trauma, like a bump, a cut, even a tight blood pressure cuff.

Oh, you know what else causes trauma to a body? Radiation.

The prospect of having a permanently swollen arm, potentially worsening over time, became a nightmare.

Yet, my burgeoning resilience whispered a mantra in my ear, "You were made for this."

As luck would have it, the hospital where I was receiving my radiation had a department dedicated to physical therapy. Within it, a skilled woman specialized in treating lymphedema.

So, my radiation adventure took on a new pattern. Three times a week, post-radiation, I'd journey to another section of the sprawling hospital: the PT department.

On occasions when there was a gap between the two sessions, the hospital's serene patio became my refuge. Adorned with a calming waterfall and lovely umbrellas, it was the perfect spot to relax, soak in the sun, and rejuvenate. This setting also provided a backdrop for some live Facebook sessions, a platform where I continued to document and share my journey with my community. The tranquil ambiance also inadvertently became a makeshift office, enabling me to ensure that my clients remained attended to.

The savior during this phase was my physical therapist, Lisa. Her vast knowledge on the subject was both comforting and enlightening. She clarified that while the risk of permanent swelling existed, it wasn't a sealed fate. Early intervention could halt its progression and possibly reverse it.

What a relief to learn this!

Our weekly sessions included meticulously wrapping my arm in bandages designed to reduce the swelling. Lisa also recommended a set of exercises to practice at home.

It felt surreal. Here I was, someone who, not too long ago, was committed to rigorous daily workouts, now navigating these entry-level movements. Adopting a beginner's mindset wasn't easy, but with each small improvement, I learned to find joy.

During one PT session, as I lifted my arm for a stretch, Lisa remarked with amusement about a "new" muscle she noticed.

"That's really cute," she said.

I bit back the urge to tell her it wasn't new for me to build muscles.

In due time and with consistent effort, my arm regained its normalcy. What a delight to experience the body's incredible adaptability.

Phew!

WHINE NOT?

Each weekday for six weeks, I visited the hospital to undergo radiation treatments. After a few weeks, I saw changes in my skin—bright reddening, followed by a fiery burn, and eventually, peeling. After the chemo side effects, these changes felt like a reprieve.

Even as the side effects of radiation became more pronounced, I felt a shade better each day. With each radiation session, I distanced myself from the toxins of chemotherapy. The discomfort of the burns seemed like a minor inconvenience compared to the draining sickness chemo produced. It's amazing how perspective can change when you've been through the worst.

As I navigated this phase of my journey, I became deeply entrenched in the art of seeking silver linings, unearthing the hidden gems.

In other words, turning whine into *shine*.

These positive angles are essential to reclaiming our narratives and "righting" our stories. And by focusing on the brighter aspects, not only do we uplift ourselves, but we inspire those around us.

For example, the ongoing thinning of my eyebrows helped me discover another creative outlet. Before this, using eyebrow products had always been a skill that eluded me. Now, I had the blessing of a blank canvas every morning. Drawing in my brows became a fun challenge, and with every stroke, I felt empowered and beautiful.

The daily commute to the hospital could have been a reason to whine, but for me, it served as a perfect opportunity to shine. This was a forced hiatus, detaching me from the demands of work and home. Those hours weren't lost; they were reclaimed, giving me space to breathe, reflect, and recalibrate. How lucky was I to have this excuse to take time every day for mental rejuvenation?

The places where cancer led me weren't on any travel bucket list. Hospitals, treatment centers, therapy sessions were not glamorous hotspots. Yet they teemed with the most beautiful human experiences. In these unlikely places, I formed bonds, shared stories, and grew in more ways than I could ever have anticipated. Whether it was trading headscarf styles or swapping recipes, every interaction was a lesson, a story, a silver lining.

On my final day of radiation, I wanted to give back a little to the people who had become a part of this journey with me. So I stopped at a local bakery and ordered a box of freshly made custom donuts. I was so excited to watch my new friends enjoy them.

And then, the moment I had been waiting for arrived. I didn't get this closure at chemo, but here I was led to a bell.

The bell is such an iconic symbol of the conclusion of cancer treatments, and I felt emotional as I reached toward the ringer.

Of course, I made sure one of the nurses was filming on my phone so I could share the event.

See the video at www.actuallyicanbook.com

Want your own Silver Lining blueprint? Uncover hidden positives in any situation with our exclusive Hidden Gems app. Access it at www.actuallyicanbook.com

BREAST CANCER AWARENESS MONTH

That October was Breast Cancer Awareness Month. Well, actually every October since 1985 is Breast Cancer Awareness Month. But this was the first year I felt compelled to spread awareness.

It's Breast Cancer Awareness Month, so it's a great reminder to ME to remind YOU... please please PLEASE get your girls checked. 💋 💕

Nika Stewart ✓
October 27, 2020 · 🌐

Pssssst.... Hey! Just reminding you - before Breast Cancer Awareness Month is over...
Get your BOO-bies checked! 🎃 👻

Pssssst.... Hey! Just reminding you - before Breast Cancer Awareness Month is over...

Get your BOO-bies checked! 👻

 **Nika Stewart** ✓
October 31, 2020 · 🌐   ···

Stop taking things so seriously!

Yes, we have things to work on. Yes, we have challenges to overcome. Yes, things may be tough.

But everything is easier and more joyous when you find the humor. Laugh at yourself sometimes.

Happy Halloween! 🎃

Stop taking things so seriously!

Yes, we have things to work on. Yes, we have challenges to overcome. Yes, things may be tough.

But everything is easier and more joyous when you find the humor. Laugh at yourself sometimes.

Happy Halloween! 🎃

Nika Stewart
November 11, 2021

How many different pieces of fruit do I need to use to get you to make that appointment? Because I can go on for days.

CHECK your girls!

P.S. I know my last photo included pumpkins, which are not a fruit. Oh my gourd - get over it 😵

How many different pieces of fruit do I need to use to get you to make that appointment? Because I can go on for days.

CHECK your girls!

P.S. I know my last photo included pumpkins, which are not a fruit. Oh my gourd - get over it 😵

UNDER RE-CONSTRUCTION

With radiation over, I could start planning my reconstruction. But this process wasn't as straightforward as one might assume.

Obviously.

I would have to wait at least six months before the doctor would entertain the thought of exchanging my expanders for implants. However, the radiation, while a lifesaver, had significant consequences. It could make it difficult for the skin and muscles to accept the implant properly.

And even if the replacement procedure went smoothly, a gamut of potential future complications loomed, including "capsular contracture."

What is capsular contracture, you ask?

When you get breast implants, your body naturally forms scar tissue around them. It's like your body's way of creating a snug pocket to hold the implant in place. Normally, this is great because it helps keep everything in position. But sometimes this scar tissue gets super tight and starts squeezing the implant. Not only can this change how the implant looks, making it appear unnatural or even misshapen, but it can also be uncomfortable or even painful.

Radiation, I was told, can greatly increase the risk of developing capsular contracture.

One solution was to bypass the use of foreign material entirely and instead move fat and blood vessels from my stomach, an intensive procedure known as DIEP Flap. But a quick assessment revealed I didn't have an adequate reservoir of fat to furnish two full breasts.

An alternative was to use a combination of my tissue and implants. Yet, this seemed counterintuitive to me. Why embark on an intricate surgery only to fall back on implants?

Another option was to move a muscle from my back—the latissimus dorsi muscle—to replace the damaged radiated muscle over my breast. The latissimus nourishes the radiated skin and is more likely to allow a smooth transition to implants.

This also felt extreme.

Enter an innovative solution. The plastic surgeon introduced a method still in its nascent stages. The concept was simple yet profound: rejuvenate the radiation-impaired area with my own stem cells. By transplanting minuscule fragments of fat from other parts of my body to the affected region, the hope was to offer healing to the damaged tissue. This enhanced healing would then, theoretically, offer a more conducive environment for the implant.

With this approach, we would schedule the procedure, and the subsequent implant replacement would be planned for six months later, ample time for the region to assimilate the cells and mend itself.

This proposal resonated with me, aligning with my belief in embracing alternative paths. So, with hope renewed and a spirit of anticipation, we earmarked a date for the first operation.

And I began to dream of perky new boobs.

A few days before this exciting procedure, I drove to the office for my pre-op appointment. Because of the whole Covid hoopla, I had to park, call into the office, and wait for the green light to come inside.

I dialed their number, rehearsing the usual pleasantries in my mind. But when I said, "Hi, I'm in the parking lot," the voice on the other end sounded, well . . . bewildered.

Why was she so confused?

"Umm, just come on in," she finally said.

I sauntered in and was quickly escorted to a treatment room, where I sat for a few minutes waiting for some grand revelation.

Finally, a nurse burst in, looking harried and embarrassed.

"Didn't you get our message?" she asked.

Umm, no.

Had I ignored a request to reschedule our appointment? Did I misunderstand the plan? Was their message sent as a smoke signal that I couldn't decode?

Spoiler alert: none of the above.

Someone in the office mentioned a mythical tale about me having a full mailbox, but I checked my phone, and nope, that wasn't true. They simply spaced on the call.

The message they were supposed to send me?

Doctor's down with Covid. Surgery is on hold.

So the reconstruction episode got a "to be continued" tag.

Was this another scene in my resilience-building saga? Challenge accepted, universe!

But, you know, a heads-up would've been nice.

CURVEBALLS AND COMEBACKS

A mix of disappointment, frustration, and honest-to-goodness worry swamped me when I heard my surgeon had contracted the virus. In the bigger scheme of things, my surgery could wait. I told the staff to please wish her a swift recovery, and I sent positive energy her way.

Driving home, I realized I was likely going to wait a long time for my procedure to be rescheduled. When the doc was healthy and back to work, she'd need to make up for lost time and fit in a lot of missed surgeries. Obviously, there were patients who were in more desperate need than me.

Fast-forward a week, just when I was beginning to pivot my attention elsewhere (learning TikTok trends and trying out new eyebrow techniques), my phone buzzed with unexpected news. My doctor was back in action, and she was keen to pencil me in. Pronto.

Oh my goodness - after accepting that my reconstruction wasn't going to start for at least a few months, I got a call today asking if I wanted to take an open appointment this Wednesday!

So I ran to the hospital for a pre-op Covid test and a chest X-ray. Then I came home and made myself this shirt.

I'm nervous and so excited. Let this journey begin!

And so, as 2020 drew to a close, I headed back to the operating table, optimistic about the chapter ahead.

Little did I know, this reconstruction story was going to have several more exciting plot twists.

BRALESS TO FLAWLESS

As 2021 dawned, the world found itself at a hopeful crossroads. The dark, uncertain days of 2020 had taken a toll on everyone, but with the introduction of the Covid vaccine, there was a renewed sense of optimism in the air.

Some old routines began to re-emerge, albeit cautiously. People started dreaming of close embraces, shared laughter, and gatherings without the omnipresent cloud of fear (or masks!).

While the world had been trying to adapt to so many new normals, there was now an underlying feeling that we were on the brink of reclaiming something precious we'd lost—not just our routines, but our sense of connection.

As establishments opened and families reunited, the year promised new beginnings. A collective resilience emerged from the previous year's challenges, and I saw so many people rewriting their stories, each with its unique blend of hope and gratitude.

Amidst this global backdrop of rediscovery, my personal journey was also moving forward. Come mid-year, it would be time for my reconstruction, a milestone that felt perfectly aligned with the world's vibes.

Over the previous eighteen months living with the tissue expanders, I had become used to an unexpected but glorious perk—the joy of going braless.

Yes, those expanders, sewn in and immovable, meant I could flaunt a skimpy tank top and even go jogging sans bra. How's that for turning whine into *shine*?

But of course I anticipated the switch to silicone implants with eagerness, knowing they'd usher in a new phase of comfort and self-assuredness.

This reconstruction surgery symbolized the end of my journey! The grand curtain call, the final bow, my moment of triumph. I was on the cusp of attaining my reward, those prized perky boobs that had occupied my thoughts for so long.

So why, then, was there a twist of melancholy in my excitement? Why was the thought of closure tinged with sadness?

It was counterintuitive, really.

The journey had been transformational in ways I never could have imagined. And now, on the precipice of what many considered the "end," I felt like I was parting with a cherished piece of myself, bidding adieu to my season of growth, challenges, and undeniable empowerment. It felt as if I was breaking up with my buddy Adventure.

As I healed from the surgery, I reminded myself that adventures don't need to conclude because one chapter ends. They can evolve and morph into different experiences.

With that realization, my first post-surgery mission was set.

Diving headfirst into reconstruction shopping, embracing the joy of finding outfits that celebrated my rejuvenated self.

After all, perky boobs deserve special clothes to show them off.

Today I did a little post-reconstruction celebrating…

"I'm about to try on some shirts for my new girls!

(some don't fit over the girls) 🎀

Might as well try some pants, too… and dresses.

Okay, I'll take it all! (just kidding)

For more inspiration and practical tools tailored to your journey, visit www.actuallyicanbook.com *and unlock a world of empowering resources.*

BACK TO THE FRONT

A few months after my reconstruction, I noticed the implant on my radiated side was getting hard. Instead of healing as a soft, natural-looking breast, it felt and looked like a lumpy rock. In most shirts, it appeared like I had shoved a tissue into my bra and it was all uneven.

I had a deformed boob. (but enough about Rob 🎀)

It wasn't just about how it looked. It felt uncomfortable, some days painful. And it seemed that it would only continue to get worse.

When the discomfort and odd appearance became too much, I had to reconsider my options. Originally, I had chosen the least intensive route—simply replacing the expanders with implants. It was the most straightforward approach at the time, but we were well aware of the potential risks. And now, it was clear we needed a more reliable solution.

After researching and considering all possible options, I landed on Lat Flap surgery. In this procedure, the latissimus dorsi muscle, which sits in the back just below the shoulder, is repurposed to aid in breast reconstruction.

The surgeon takes this muscle, along with some skin and fat, and moves it to the chest. The entire process is intricate, because they need to ensure the relocated tissue receives an adequate blood supply.

Essentially, I was going to move a back muscle to the front of my body.

This procedure would leave scars on my back, but they would likely be in a spot generally covered by a bra strap. It wasn't just about aesthetics, though. This surgery offered hope for a more comfortable and natural-feeling result.

The surgery would reintroduce me to expanders, reminiscent of the experience that started it all—my mastectomy.

The expanders would be in for three months, prepping the area for the final implants. And as I had done the first time, I'd visit the doctor every two weeks to fill the expanders with fluid, gradually stretching them to accommodate the size I wanted.

But the biggest challenge?

The drains.

Remember how awful it was dealing with those three drains after the mastectomy? This procedure would send me home with six.

Six drains!

It felt overwhelming, to say the least. But I decided this was the procedure I needed.

After a three-day hospital stay, I went home to deal with the six tubes protruding from my body, channeling fluid into rubber bulbs.

Thrice daily, I found myself with the task of cleaning out these tubes, emptying those bulbs, gauging the liquid, and jotting down the measurements. As you can imagine, handling this is no walk in the park, especially when you're worn out, your vision is fuzzy, and you're grappling with pain.

But then, something funny happened.

After nine days, when the doctor removed half of the drains, having only three felt like a relief.

Three drains? Piece of cake!

It's funny how our perspective changes when faced with a bigger challenge.

Healing from this surgery was more difficult than the others because of how extensive it was. My recovery demanded patience. But you know me—I made a plan to make my recovery time as enjoyable as I could. So, I relaxed in bed and caught up on a few shows. And I worked on my laptop in bed. And I enjoyed milkshakes and Dunkin' twisty breads.

I wasn't allowed to drive for about a month, but after a few weeks I felt well enough for an outing. As luck would have it, Ellie was now seventeen and had her driver's license. So she played chauffeur, taking us out to a fun destination: Target. Spending extra time with her was one of the best silver linings.

Fast forward three months. As the expanders made way for

the implants, I dared hope that my reconstructive journey had reached its destination.

Yet, with every step, or, more precisely, every stair I climbed with my laptop, my body introduced me to a quirky feature—a contracting muscle in a rather unconventional location.

While I think most of us are oblivious to the subtle contractions of the latissimus dorsi muscle, the first time I felt it twitch in my breast, oh, I noticed it. It is such a strange sensation!

I'm guessing over time I'll probably get used to it.

Embracing the Endless Marathon

If there's one big shift in how I see things now, it's that I'm no longer waiting for the "finish line" on this journey.

From the moment I was diagnosed, my life was transformed irreversibly. This adventure is never over, from follow-up appointments, to scans, to potential surgeries to fix challenges, this is my new normal.

The emotional and psychological shifts have changed who I am. And I cherish it. Now I live with a consistent tightness in my chest and my arms don't reach as far. But my silhouette? Perkier than ever, with the added bonus of a bra-free lifestyle!

And there's my *shine*.

GOOD NEWS, BAD NEWS

One of my favorite parables, which I've often leaned on during my journey, is that of an Asian farmer.

There was a farmer in China who was blessed with a horse, a gift many in his village envied. But, as unpredictable as life can be, the horse ran away.

His neighbor hurried over, tut-tutting in sympathy. "That's such bad news."

The farmer simply shrugged. "Good news? Bad news? Who really knows?"

Imagine the surprise when the horse not only returned but brought with it a companion!

The village was abuzz with whispers of the farmer's good fortune. But the farmer remained unfazed, repeating, "Good news? Bad news? Who really knows?"

He gifted the second horse to his son. One day, as his son rode the new horse, he was thrown off, breaking his leg quite badly.

The same sympathetic neighbor rushed over, shaking his head, "What terrible luck!" Yet, the farmer's response remained unchanged.

"Good news? Bad news? Who really knows?"

Soon after, a decree from the emperor arrived. All able-bodied young men were to be conscripted into the army for a war. Every heart in the village grew heavy with dread. But the farmer's son, with his broken leg, was exempt. The tides of fortune had turned again.

Was this good news? Who really knows?

Life is an unpredictable journey, filled with events that are immediately christened as *setbacks* or *blessings*. And when we conclude that something is good or bad, we consider that a fact.

We intuitively label circumstances as positive or negative, lucky or unlucky, but these judgments are often incomplete. It's like reading a book and declaring the entire plot based on one chapter. In many scenarios, only the passage of time can uncover the full spectrum of an event's significance.

Or perhaps we don't have to wait to see if our life events are good or bad. Maybe we get to decide for ourselves.

"You have cancer."

Is this good news? Bad news?

I get to make that choice. Because actually, I can!

Here's why it is GOOD news.

The very diagnosis that we are taught spells doom, actually unlocked doors I hadn't even known existed.

With each medical appointment, therapy session, and social

media share, I wasn't just navigating an illness, I was crafting a vibrant tapestry, cultivating relationships, and making an impact in ways I'd never imagined.

Being diagnosed with cancer had ironically granted me a platform. I was now in a position to spread awareness, champion causes, and advocate for those in need. I discovered that a singular event in my life had ripples that reached further than I'd ever expected.

The day I was invited by the Susan G. Komen Foundation to share my story at a charity softball tournament was one of those incredible opportunities.

In front of hundreds of people, I talked about Susan G. Komen and shared their incredible message, mission, and resources, from their helpline to available financial aid. And I got to throw out the first pitch!

So okay, maybe the ball didn't sail straight over home plate. I never claimed to be a starting pitcher. Plus, I was just six weeks out from another reconstruction surgery, so I wasn't able to stretch my arm very well.

Excuses aside, that pitch was a symbol of hope. As I stood on the mound with the weight of that pink ball in my hand (and then took a few steps forward so I had a better chance of actually reaching the catcher with my throw!), I felt the weight of my responsibility, too. I wasn't just representing myself, but all those who had faced or were facing this diagnosis.

As the ball soared through the air, traveling awkwardly to the right of home plate, it carried with it my message that adversity can lead to profound strength, and pain can be transformed into purpose.

I hope that poor catcher got the message as she lurched to the side to try to catch the flyaway ball!

Another heartwarming experience happened a few months earlier when I got a text from a neighbor. She shared a photo of her older daughter who I had met just once before she went to college on a softball scholarship. In the photo, I saw a pink softball shirt with my last name on it.

At first I thought she had snapped a pic of one of the players on her daughter's team to show me that someone had my name.

But then I read her text:

Hi Nika. We are headed home from a softball game at Ava's college. Today was the breast cancer awareness day. Her suitemate's mom, who is currently battling BC, threw the 1st pitch. Each player honored a brave strong individual they know that battled BC. We had a convo last month about who we knew. I mentioned my aunt and of course your story. She was touched. She chose to honor you! AND they won both games against rider.

I assumed she would pick my aunt lol! but she was so inspired by your fight and strength and your relationship with your daughter the whole time.

I'm glad she picked you and hope you know how you've impacted so many in a positive way!

The next time I went to their house, Ava was home, and she gave me the beautiful pink softball shirt with my name on it. I wore that shirt to throw out the pitch at the Susan G. Komen charity event!

Online, people continually reach out. Some share their own stories, others seek advice, and a few simply want to chat. I am frequently told, "You inspired me to find my own happy moments, even when things seemed really tough."

Their words warm my heart and prove to me the importance of sharing the journey.

Each interaction, hug, comment, and heartfelt conversation reinforces my philosophy—It's not the events in our life that define us, but how we choose to perceive and respond to them.

The diagnosis of cancer, which could have been a deep well of despair, instead became a bridge connecting me to countless souls, uniting us in shared experiences and resilience.

Each day is sewn with threads of every hue, dark and light. And while the dark threads may seem dominant at times, it's our perspective that determines the feel of the final cloth. I choose to see the beauty in those intertwined threads and try to inspire others to embrace it all and find their own patterns of joy.

Rob recently asked me a question, and he was shocked by my answer. He said, "If you could go back in time and erase the fact that you ever had cancer, would you?"

Without needing to think about my answer, I blurted out, "No. I wouldn't change a thing."

When I first received my diagnosis, I was worried, and as my journey started and continued, I faced many rough patches along the way. Additionally, my body was permanently transformed by my experience. But like the Asian farmer, I cannot say my cancer journey was "bad news," as so much good came from it. Not only did I strengthen my confidence and resilience, but I touched the lives of so many in the process.

Not every setback is ultimately a bad experience. How we deal with our challenges helps to shape and define us. And while I do not want to go through that experience again, I would not take it all back, even if I magically had the opportunity to do so.

CREATING YOUR OWN MILESTONES

One year ago today…

I was nervously waiting for results of my biopsy. When the email came (yes, an email), I saw words I didn't really understand, but knew didn't sound good.

So I googled, and I learned that my diagnosis was not bad at all. Very simple, and easily treated.

Unfortunately the biopsy had been done wrong, and over the next few weeks, each new test and result revealed worse news.

However, one year after that first email, I want to celebrate. I want to celebrate the completion of my double mastectomy, chemotherapy, and radiation. And I want to celebrate getting my energy back. And I want to celebrate being cancer-free.

I want to celebrate by having all my friends and family over for a big party, with hugs and dancing and laughing and cake.

But instead, I'll celebrate—with my little family of 3—by playing games, watching a movie, and maybe having a glass of wine.

Thank you, my beautiful Facebook friends, for cheering me on, inspiring me, and making me laugh this year.

Life has a peculiar way of denying us the clichéd storybook endings we often yearn for.

As I counted down my chemotherapy sessions, I awaited that defining moment of closure, the metaphorical finish line. Many visualize it as the traditional bell ringing, a clear, crisp sound echoing one's triumph over the grueling challenges of treatment.

For me, that ending note remained elusive.

Not because they didn't have a bell ceremony at my treatment center. I don't even think that would have felt like a true celebration, because I was alone and the jubilation I dreamed of included family and friends.

During the early stages of my diagnosis, I envisioned a grand celebration at the end of my treatment. This would be the well-earned finale to my ordeal, where I could revel in the triumph of my experience. I kept this celebration in the back of my mind. It often gave me the inspiration and courage I needed to get through my sessions.

But as the pandemic progressed, it meant I couldn't gather my cheering squad around me. The absence of their physical presence created a void, and the anticipated fanfare turned into a silent, lingering yearning.

I had the privilege of ringing a bell at the end of my radiation, a small semblance of the traditional closure. Yet, my heart still yearned for more, for that grand celebration of resilience and accomplishment.

With the advent of vaccines and the world cautiously limping back to normalcy, the thought of throwing a party frequently crossed my mind. This would be a celebration, not just of my triumph, but also a heartfelt tribute to all the amazing people who'd journeyed with me.

But as life often does, it got busy, and this became yet another thought bookmarked for later.

Yet, month after month, a nagging feeling would revisit. And every time I thought about it, I teared up. I knew this meant it was important, a necessary acknowledgment of the past and the challenges overcome. I desperately craved this celebration. I needed to honor the journey—mine and of all those who walked it with me.

But here's the thing. Milestones don't have to be traditional or expected. They're deeply personal.

And that's where the "*Actually, I Can*" philosophy kicked in for me. I realized if the world wasn't going to provide the closure, the ceremony I needed, I had the power and every right to craft my own. Not for vanity, not for the show, but for my soul's deep desire to acknowledge, celebrate, and find peace.

And a little for vanity.

And who am I kidding? Of course, it also had to be a show.

But it wasn't just about me. So many had been on this journey alongside me, vicariously living the highs and lows, sending their prayers, love, and strength. My need for a celebration was also about honoring their emotional investment, their extreme generosity, their unwavering support.

Three years after my final chemo treatment, I finally made plans for a gala. It felt like an exercise in reclaiming power.

In life, where so much is out of our control, creating my milestone became an act of assertion, proof of my freedom.

It was a statement: "I decide how this chapter concludes."

~~~

As I planned the party, I realized that, of course, I was turning this into another obsession, another outlet to give me space for joy and creativity, to remind myself of the beauty and fun I can choose.

And what fun I chose!

The party would be a celebration of resilience and gratitude. The signature pink drink (the No Mo Chemo-Tini); the pink candy cart filled with gumballs, lollipops, and pink chocolate coins; the dessert buffet filled with pink cupcakes, cookies, and dips.

My biggest obsession? The cupcakes. I wanted these to be a big thank you to each of my family and friends—a beautiful, delicious bite of gratitude from me.

I designed what I wanted it to look like, not only the cupcake itself, but the presentation of it. I purchased champagne flutes that I would fill with pink candy and place the pretty cupcakes on top.

I ordered four dozen custom treats from a local bakery. Golden cake with several shades of pink frosting and pearl sprinkles. This was to be the pièce de résistance of the party. I put so much planning into these cupcakes, and I placed so much importance on them.

But perhaps it had been too long. Although in the months leading up to the party, I was still healing from reconstruction surgeries, it was now three years since my cancer diagnosis and my most difficult treatments. Maybe I needed to be reminded of my philosophy.

So, on the morning of the gala, as I excitedly picked up the forty-eight cupcakes from the bakery and placed them in the back seat of my car, I was a little distracted. And as I pulled out of the parking lot and slowed down at a traffic light, I heard the box slide forward.

As I turned to look, I saw through the plastic box that all the cupcakes had merged into one giant mess.

I wish I could say that I immediately saw the humor.

Instead, I screamed in agony. I screamed and cried as I drove the next few miles home. I felt that if I could scream loud enough, I could rewind time. So, I kept screaming.

When I got home, I cried to Rob. He did everything he could to help me feel better, telling me he'd drive all over town looking for similar cupcakes, offering suggestions of what we could serve instead. But I was inconsolable. And I had to clean and set up for the guests who would arrive in a few hours.

A while later, as I was decorating the dessert table with candy, Rob asked if he should bring the ruined cupcakes in from the car.

I said, "Why would you bring them in? Throw them in the trash."

But then suddenly I remembered to turn whine into *shine*.

I placed the box of ruined cupcakes on the table and unwrapped each one, dumping everything—smooshed cake, frosting, and pearl sprinkles—into a large bowl. Then I blended it all together.

The resulting dip was the most delicious dessert at the party!

For entertainment, I compiled a reel of my social media posts throughout my journey. The posts, videos, and comments provided my guests with a brief capsule of my experience, running the gamut of feelings from shock and depression to exhilaration and ecstasy.

This video was so very personal and packed with emotion. I am now planning to use it as a backdrop during my presentations.

You can see the full video at www.actuallyicanbook.com

PLAYING GAMES

Rob, of course, had a little surprise up his sleeve. Wanting to sprinkle a touch of fun and intrigue into the mix, he handed out index cards and asked every guest to write a little-known fact about themselves. A secret, an odd talent, an unexpected childhood story—something I'd have never guessed.

During the party, amidst all the laughter and merriment, he read them out loud, turning the floor into a delightful guessing game.

Who could've possibly gotten caught stealing when they were in middle school? Who competed in the Miss Teen New Jersey pageant? Whose parents secretly whispered to them (often) that he was their favorite? (Oh, that was my brother.)

The revelations led to giggles, gasps, and a whole lot of playful banter.

Then, just as I thought the game had run its course, Rob read out a rather touching note. "What you don't know: How much I admire your strength, outlook on life, and your shining spirit. You have inspired many people to live better."

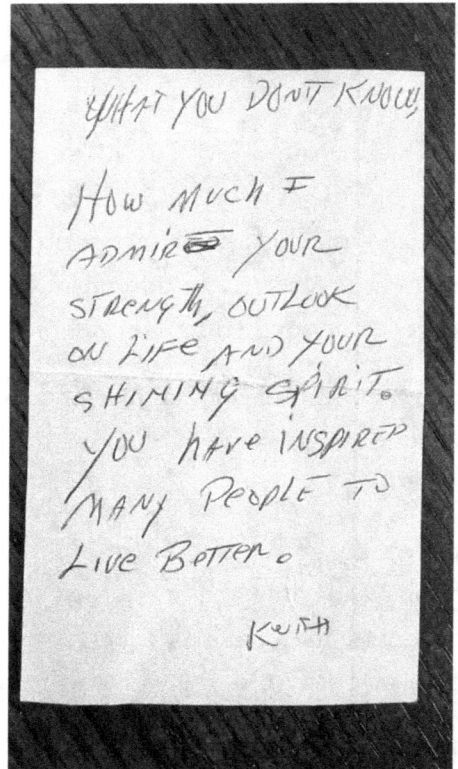

There was a momentary pause. An emotional hush fell over the room. Instead of making me guess, Rob revealed, "That was your dad."

My heart swelled. But before the moment could fully sink in, my dad, always the prankster, chimed in, "You read the wrong side!"

Rob looked confused, but then flipped the card, took a breath, and read with mock seriousness:

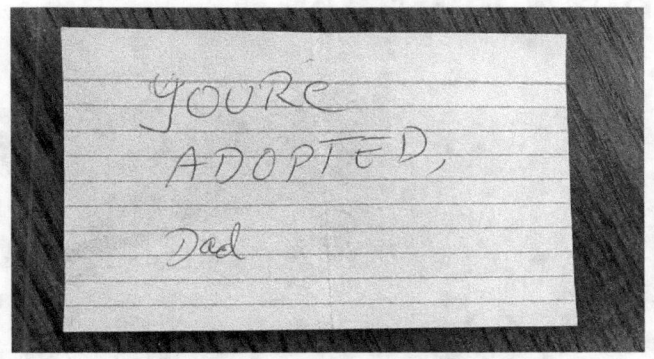

The room erupted in laughter.

Coming soon: Actually I Can: The Counterintuitive Approach to Unexpectedly Learning You are Adopted When You are 55 Years Old

Keep the momentum going!
For more inspiration and practical tools,
exercises, and videos, visit www.actuallyicanbook.com
to unlock a world of empowering resources.

ABOUT THE AUTHOR

Meet Nika Stewart: Social media trailblazer, heart-centered entrepreneur, dedicated mom, part-time rock star, and resilient soul who turned her cancer journey into a viral phenomenon, brimming with hope, laughter, and unyielding positivity.

Living and thriving in Central New Jersey with her hysterically funny writer husband; her bright, creative, compassionate, fun-loving, beautiful-inside-and-out daughter; and her thinks-she's-a-dog kitty cat, Nika enjoys running her business coaching club, experimenting with margarita flavors, researching the perfect lipstick (it still eludes her), and creating viral YouTube videos.

Her infectious energy and story of resilience make her a popular speaker for audiences seeking inspiration and practical strategies for embracing life's curveballs and finding joy in adversity.

A lifelong musician, Nika is the lead singer of Backtrack, a rock cover band, and serves as a Cantor at her temple during the High Holidays.